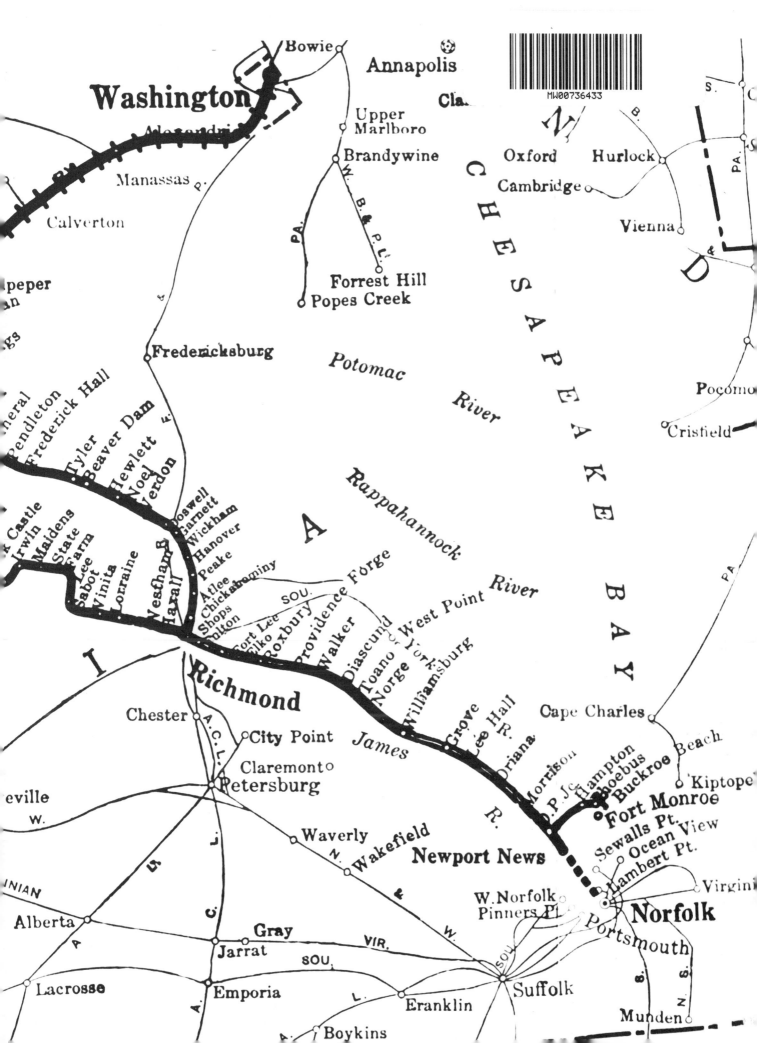

Virginia Railroads
Volume 2: Chesapeake & Ohio
Thomas W. Dixon, Jr.

Published 2011 by
TLC Publishing Inc.
18292 Forest Rd.
Forest, Virginia 24551
434-385-4076
www.tlcrailroadbooks.com

TLC Publishing Inc.
18292 Forest Rd.
Forest, Virginia 24551
434-385-4076
www.tlcrailroadbooks.com

ISBN 978-0939487516

Digital Photo Production, Design, and Layout
by
Karen Parker

Printed in the U.S.A. by
Walsworth Print Group, Marceline, Mo.

Front Cover: Streamlined C&O L-1 4-6-4 Hudson type No. 493 with passenger train No. 47, The Sportsman, departing Main Street Station in Richmond in October, 1952. (Photo by J. I. Kelly, C&O Historical Society Collection, COHS-103, Colorized by Karen Parker)

Title Page: Three EMD E8s power No. 4, The Sportsman, as it passes the little Afton depot near the top of the Blue Ridge grade in about 1960, with 13 cars in consist, including two mail storage, a full RPO, express and baggage, plus coaches, sleepers, and a business car bringing up the rear. (W. E. Warden, Jr. Photo)

Facing Page: Virginia's geography is varied, but the Blue Ridge helps to define the state as is runs diagonally northeast to southwest. Here C&O J-2 class 4-8-2 Mountain type No. 548 is powering local passenger, mail, and express train No. 104 in July 1949. Crossing the Blue Ridge was one of C&O's consistent challenges through the years. (J. I. Kelly photo, C&O Historical Society Collection, COHS-335)

Back End Sheets: Two passenger-equipped K-4 2-8-4 Kanawhas (2763 and 2761) a heavy train makes its way west near Swoope, ready to assault the North Mountain grade in about 1949. (C&O Ry. Photo, C&O Historical Society Collection, CSPR-2356)

Back Cover Top Left: K-3a No. 2324 is bringing a coal train off the James River Viaduct at Richmond into Fulton Yard. It has taken the heavy train down the descending gradient of the James River and Rivanna Subdivisions from Clifton Forge. The train will get new power at Fulton and go the last 85 miles to Newport News. (Photo by Carl Tordella, Karen Parker Collection)

Back Cover Top Right: GP9 No. 6045 and two mates are headed out of Clifton Forge yard toward the James River line toward Richmond and Newport News (to the left behind the photographer) with a heavy coal train in 1956. Cabooses stored at right are for use on trains going up the Mountain Subdivision, out of sight behind the photographer to the right. (C&O Ry. Photo, C&O Historical Society Collection, CSPR-CL606)

Back Cover Center Left: In this ca. 1958 photo, the collier Crystal Sapphire, out of London, is taking on coal at C&O Pier 15 at Newport News. The hopper car has just been emptied in the rotary dumper and is coasting up a steep incline from which it will gain momentum to roll back into the empty yard. (C&O Ry. Photo, C&O Historical Society Collection, CSPR-CL829)

Back Cover Center Right: Rail Diesel Car No. 9060 leads two others at the Gordonsville station in September 1958. After arrival of No. 4, The Sportsman (seen in background on the Washington Subdivision side of the station), it will take the coach passengers down the Piedmont and Peninsula Subdivisions. For a short while these cars were used as the Virginia Section of certain trains and were called "Chessieliners." (Gene Huddleston Photo)

Back Cover Bottom: Train No. 4, the eastbound Sportsman, led by E8 4028 and two others rolls through the rural countryside near Goshen in September 1967. Mill Mountain is in the background. This is just eight months before the train was discontinued. The practice of using three E8s was standard for trains between Charlottesville, Va. and Ashland, Ky. From 1958 until the end. (Gene Huddleston Photo)

Table of Contents

Introduction 4

1 : Norfolk, Newport News, and the Peninsula Subdivision 9

2 : Richmond 27

3 : The Piedmont Subdivision 35

4 : The Washington Subdivision 43

5 : Charlottesville 49

6 : The Rivanna Subdivision 56

7 : Gladstone 69

8 : The James River Subdivision 71

9 : The Mountain Subdivision 82

10 : Clifton Forge 97

11: The Alleghany Subdivision 106

12 : Passenger Service... 119

Introduction

This is the second in a series of books about railroads in the Commonwealth of Virginia. The first volume (published 2010), gives an overview of all the major railways with lines in Virginia and summarizes their history along with treatment of important short lines as well. This volume will deal with the Chesapeake & Ohio, which originated, and was headquartered in Virginia for many years.

The Chesapeake & Ohio was one of the nation's major railroad systems that had its origins in Virginia, and was very closely associated with the Commonwealth during a large portion of its existence. Its early existence as the Virginia Central was contained entirely within what is today Virginia, but after the War Between the States it expanded through what was previously the trans-Alleghany region of the old state, which after 1863 had become West Virginia. In the modern era, C&O expanded to Cincinnati, Chicago, Louisville, and Toledo in the west and Washington and Newport News in the east. After absorption of the Pere Marquette Railway it had numerous lines in Michigan and Ontario. It became most widely known for its coal traffic from the rich bituminous fields of southern West Virginia and eastern Kentucky, and for a long time in the mid-20th Century it was the world's largest originator of bituminous coal. In the early 1960s it joined the ancient Baltimore & Ohio in what was a merger all but in name, and in the 1972 the C&O, B&O, and Western Maryland joined to become Chessie System Railroads. In 1987 Chessie System merged with Seaboard System, which was an amalgam of southeastern railroads including the Atlantic Coast Line, Seaboard Air Line, Louisville & Nashville, Clinchfield, Georgia, and other lines, to form today's giant CSX system.

The Chesapeake & Ohio's earliest predecessor line was the Louisa Railroad. The company was chartered by the Virginia General Assembly on February 18, 1836. Because the state subscribed a portion of the stock it was allowed to appoint two (later three) of the five directors, thus giving it a very strong influence on the line, which proved to be beneficial to the new railway in most respects. Frederick Harris of Frederick Hall in Louisa County, was elected the first president, serving until 1841 when he was succeeded by Charles Y. Kimbrough for a few years, and finally by Edmond Fontaine from 1845 until 1850 (and from 1850 to 1865 as president of the Virginia Central--see below).

The Louisa Railroad extended from Louisa Court House to Hanover Junction (now Doswell), where it joined the line operated by the Richmond, Fredericksburg & Potomac Railroad. RF&P connected Richmond northward to Potomac Creek where steamboat connections delivered freight and passengers to Washington and points north. In later years it was completed to Washington.

The main reason for the Louisa Railroad was to help farmers get their products to market in Richmond. The line was leased to the RF&P until 1847 when the Louisa owners began independent operations. By 1851 it was extended into Richmond (over the objections of the RF&P), and in the west reached Gordonsville and Charlottesville. In line with the new ambitions of the road it was renamed Virginia Central in 1850, with a charter to build to Covington, at the foot of the Allgehanies, where connection would be made with a state-sponsored Covington & Ohio Railroad, leading to the Ohio River.

Between 1850 and 1857 the Virginia Central was built across the Blue Ridge through the help of the state-sponsored Blue Ridge Railroad, then across the Shenandoah Valley and North Mountain to Jackson's River Station (near Clifton Forge) about nine miles short of Covington. Here construction stopped and the War Between the States intervened.

Virginia Central was a very important Confederate supply line during the war, carrying huge amounts of goods and troops. It also was actually used in tactical operations. By the end of the war the railroad was badly damaged, yet by late 1865 was back in operation. The owners wanted to extend westward, and in 1869 were able to interest Collis P. Huntington to back the venture. He was fresh from completing the Central Pacific portion of the Transcontinental Railroad and had the idea that he wanted to create a true transcontinental system under one person's control: his.

With Huntington's backing, the line, now renamed Chesapeake & Ohio, built across the wilds of the southern part of the new state of West Virginia (following the old line of the partially completed Covington & Ohio, another antebellum state venture), reaching the Ohio. The new line was opened in May 1873. Huntington's aim was to make C&O the eastern connection of his system of railroads from the west.

Initial traffic on the C&O was mainly local and consisted largely of mineral, forest, and farm products. It was not until the 1880s that coal traffic became important. It was coal that would make the C&O, and with each year that traffic grew.

In 1881 C&O built a line down the Virginia Peninsula from Richmond to Newport News, opposite Norfolk on the great Hampton Roads harbor. Here it provided a pier to transfer coal to ships and barges bound for the northwestern U. S. and overseas. The eastbound coal traffic to Newport News would be the largest portion of C&O's business until about 1920, when coal traffic moving to the industrializing Midwest began to equal or exceeded it in volume.

In the era before railroads, George Washington himself became president of the James River & Kanawha Canal with the aim of connecting Tidewater navigation with the Ohio-Mississippi system. This canal was built as far as Buchanan by 1860, but after the war railroad technology was proving so much better than canals, it fell into disfavor. The Richmond & Alleghany Railroad bought the canal and built a line from Richmond through Lynchburg to Clifton Forge along the tow-path of the canal in 1881. The R&A was bought by C&O in 1890 and from that day until the present has provided it an excellent route for eastbound coal, avoiding the heavy mountain grades of the old Virginia Central line via Staunton and Charlottesville. Because C&O bought the R&A, which succeeded the JR&K Canal, the C&O advertising men of the 1930s began calling C&O "George Washington's Railroad," since he was president of

a predecessor company. Washington also had the dream of the "Great Connection," by which the navigation on the James would be connected with the resource-rich interior by the Ohio-Mississippi systems.

By 1881 C&O had acquired Huntington's planned western connection over roads he owned via Louisville and Memphis to New Orleans, and for a brief period 1888-89 he controlled a true transcontinental, but it couldn't be held together and the C&O portion went into Vanderbilt and Morgan hands in 1889.

By the 1890s C&O's coal business was growing so rapidly that the line had to be completely rebuilt, which occurred under the new owners. They installed M. E. Ingalls, who was president of the New York Central-controlled Big Four Railroad (Cleveland, Cincinnati, Chicago & St. Louis). With the new backing the C&O was rebuilt, refurbished, and upgraded to better accommodate the booming coal traffic.

In 1889 the new owners negotiated for trackage rights over the Virginia Midland Railroad (later Southern Railway, now Norfolk Southern) from Orange, Virginia, to Washington, thus giving it access to the Northeastern railroad network. In that year C&O began its high-profile name-train passenger service from New York (via the Pennsylvania Railroad connection), and Washington to Cincinnati,

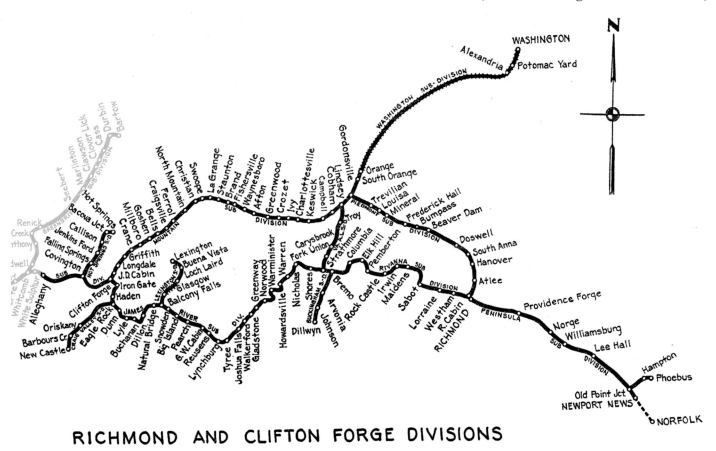

RICHMOND AND CLIFTON FORGE DIVISIONS

where connections were made via the Big Four to Chicago, Indianapolis, and St. Louis. These connections remained intact to the end of C&O-operated passenger service with Amtrak in 1971. Though passenger business remained a tiny fraction of C&O income, it lavished a great deal of money, advertising, and interest in the service in the following decades. In 1888-89 C&O completed a line along the south (Kentucky) side of the Ohio River and across that stream into Cincinnati. The first through train over the new C&O routing was the *Fast Flying Virginian*, inaugurated May 11, 1889. Of course, C&O still continued to operate passenger trains between Newport News and Charlottesville. At that point they were consolidated with trains from Washington. From Charlottesville west the consolidated train passed through southern West Virginia and was again broken up at Ashland, Kentucky, where sections went to Louisville and to Cincinnati (and to Detroit after inauguration of *The Sportsman* service in 1930). C&O also established a small yard in Norfolk and began serving that city by car float, barge, and passenger ferry from its terminal at Newport News.

In the years from 1890 to 1915, scores of branch lines were built in West Virginia and eastern Kentucky, which tapped some of the richest coal deposits in the east, and the coal business ballooned. As explained before, eastbound traffic to Newport News through Virginia, accounted for a large part of this until about 1920, when as much was moving west as east. However, both sides of the traffic continued to expand.

In 1910 the Hocking Valley Railway of Ohio was acquired, which gave C&O an outlet for its coal to the Great Lakes at Toledo. It leased trackage rights of the Louisville & Nashville to Louisville, and thus the modern C&O system was in place.

In Virginia, in 1889-90, Clifton Forge was built as a major shop area and terminal and became the eastern hub of the system, while Huntington, West Virginia and Russell, Kentucky, became the western hubs. Three major mainline subdivisions radiated from Clifton Forge. First, the old Virginia Central line, called the Mountain Subdivision, ran to Staunton, Waynesboro, and Charlottesville, where it forked again, the Piedmont Subdivision (which was the original line of the Louisa Railroad) running down to Richmond and the Washington Subdivision operating to Orange and over the Southern Railway into Washington. Second, the James River line ran along that river through Lynchburg to Richmond. Third, the Alleghany Subdivision ran westward from Clifton Forge, across Alleghany Mountain

(in this part of Virginia Alleghany is spelled with an "a") and terminated at Hinton, West Virginia

The Mountain Subdivision handled all the through passenger trains as well as fast freight headed for the Northeastern connections. The James River Line (James River and Rivanna Subdivisions) handled the eastbound coal but had only local passenger business, as well as some fast freight headed to and from the ocean terminal. The Alleghany, of course, handled all the coal, freight and passenger business to and from the west, leaving Virginia at the crest of Alleghany Mountain.

The shops at Clifton Forge did all steam locomotive repair for the eastern end of the road, and always remained the second most important mechanical repair facility on the C&O (after Huntington).

At Richmond the Piedmont Subdivision entered from the northwest, and the James River Line (Rivanna Subdivision) from the west. In 1901 a major rebuilding of terminals at Richmond resulted in the construction of the mile-and-a-half James River Viaduct, which carried C&O coal trains from the Rivanna Subdivision, avoiding the congestion of the city, to a new facility at Fulton yard, on the city's eastern edge.

As apart of this work, a large new station was built on Main Street, which accommodated C&O and Seaboard Air Line Railway passenger trains. It still stands today, largely preserved and now again host to Amtrak passenger trains operating on the old C&O line to Newport News.

Eastward from Richmond the Peninsula Subdivision ran about 85 miles to Newport News on a fairly straight alignment with good grades. It was used to get the coal trains and fast freight to Hampton Roads.

From the old Richmond & Alleghany along the James River, C&O inherited some branch lines. The Buckingham Branch ran from Bremo, (about 66 miles west of Richmond) for about 17 miles to Dillwyn, handling local agricultural and forest products, as well as soapstone and other mineral products. In the 1980s it was abandoned and was bought by the Buckingham Branch Railroad and today operates very successfully as a short line. The Buckingham Branch mainline terminal was at Strathmore, just a mile and a half west of its connection with the Rivanna Subdivision at Sabot. Strathmore was also the terminal for the Virginia Air Line Subdivision. This short line was built as an independent railroad in 1909 and ran from this point to the C&O's

Washington Subdivision at Lindsay. It was bought by C&O in 1912, and was maintained mainly as a secondary by-pass route since it originated little traffic. It was used for coal headed to Washington and points east, thus bypassing the mountain grades.

From Warren, about 85 miles west of Richmond, the Alberene Subdivision tapped soapstone deposits to the north of the C&O and was a marginal operation, lasting to the 1960s.

The Lexington Branch ran from Balcony Falls (Glasgow) to Lexington, and was mainly for local business. It was opened in 1881 just a month or so after completion of the Richmond & Allegany line. In 1905 the line was consolidated with Norfolk & Western's Shenandoah Valley line from a point near Balcony Falls to Buena Vista. The branch operated until it was washed out by a Hurricane-induced flood in the 1970s.

At Eagle Rock, about 17 miles east of Clifton Forge, the Craig Valley Branch extended 26 miles to New Castle, Virginia. It was built to carry iron ore in the era when Virginia was an important iron producer, but the deposits were not as rich as expected and the line continued its life as a local carrier occupied with a marginal traffic in agricultural and forest products. It was abandoned in 1961 and much of its right of way became a state highway.

On the Alleghany Subdivision, the Hot Springs Branch ran northward from Covington 25 miles to Hot Springs. It was built in 1890 to provide passenger service to and from the new Homestead Resort Hotel at that point. The hotel was purchased by C&O president M. E. Ingalls, and developed into one of the east's premier mountain resorts. It remains so today. The branch was mainly for passenger business, transporting through sleeping cars. These cars arrived at Clifton Forge, mainly from New York City, and were dropped there by the name trains. The cars were made up in to trains that took them up the branch to Hot Springs at convenient times and returned them to the mainline to be attached to trains operating back to Washington and New York. The branch was abandoned in 1970, spent a few years as a tourist line, and was then taken up.

The other branch from Covington was the Potts Creek Subdivision, which was another line built for iron ore extraction. Again, the expectations were false and no appreciable traffic developed. The line was built 1906-1908 and was abandoned in 1934.

Two short branch lines for Sulphur Mines and other mineral production extended from Mineral, on the Piedmont Subdivision, but were abandoned before the era of this book's emphasis.

Passenger operations were centered in Charlottesville, where the mainline name trains were broken up and consolidated. As previously mentioned, trains arriving from the west were broken with one section headed to Washington and the other Newport News, and the opposite occurred westbound.

C&O's headquarters offices were, of course, in Virginia when its lines largely operated there, and after its expansion Richmond remained as its center of operational, mechanical, engineering, and administrative control. This changed in the period 1890-1900 when the Big Four controlled, with executive and many administrative offices located in Cincinnati and Washington. About 1900 the headquarters returned to Richmond. From the 1930s onward the highest executive offices moved to Cleveland, as a result of the Van Sweringen financial control. Mechanical and engineering offices left in the early 1960s to Huntington, W. Va., and many other offices were gradually consolidated and closed, a process that was completed during the C&O/B&O merger years of he 1960s-70s. Successor CSX Corporation returned to Richmond in the 1980s, but then all its operations were eventually consolidated in Jacksonville, Florida, and the last vestiges of C&O were gone from Richmond.

C&O's lines in Virginia can be characterized as carrying the C&O's coal, freight, and passenger business through from other points. The actual traffic originated in within Virginian was much smaller than that which came from the western portions of the railway. Virginia lines served as a conduit for this large traffic. This is not to say, however, that Virginia was not important to the C&O of the mid-20th Century. It certainly was. However there was no coal on C&O lines in the commonwealth, and what traffic originated was from other products and industries, which included timber products, some other minerals, and products of factories, as well as agricultural products.

Passenger traffic was important from the several centers that C&O served, including Richmond, Newport News/Norfolk area, Alexandria and Washington, and the smaller cities of Charlottesville and Staunton.

C&O mainlines in Virginia connected with the Atlantic Coast Line, Seaboard Air Line, Richmond, Fredericksburg & Potomac, and Southern in Richmond, with the Southern Railway's main Washington-New Orleans line at Charlottesville and Lynchburg, with N&W and Southern again at Lynchburg, and various short lines, as explained later in this book.

Since the C&O originated in central Virginia and had its main operational and executive headquarters at Richmond for much of its early life, the line always considered itself a "southern" railway rather than a mid-western one, though it had many lines and much business those states, especially after the acquisition of the Chicago, Cincinnati & Louisville in 1910, control of the Hocking Valley Railway of Ohio in 1910 (and its merger in 1930), and the Pere Marquette Railway of Michigan in 1928 (and its merger in 1947), the Nickel Plate Road of New York, Ohio, and Indiana in 1923 (until it left the C&O family in 1947).

This book will treat the C&O lines in Virginia in geographical order east-to-west rather than chronological. The statically data gives will usually be based on data from 1948 when the C&O was at its height in the number of stations and lines operated in Virginia, just before the dislocations which the next two decades would bring.

Emblematic of C&O railroading in Virginia is the heavy mainline passenger train. Here a pair of E8s power the Washington section of No. 1, The George Washington, at Alexandria in 1965. It will get even bigger after it is joined by the "Virginia section" (out of Newport News and Richmond) at Charlottesville. (Jim Shaw photo)

Beautiful and varied mountain scenery is characteristic of C&O's mainline on the Mountain Subdivision between Charlottesville and Clifton Forge. Here motor car M-1535 has signal maintainers going to a job on the Mountain line near Millboro in September, 1942. (C&O Ry. Photo, C&O Historical Society Collection, CSPR-57.195)

1: Norfolk, Newport News, and the Peninsula Subdivision

This chapter covers C&O's huge terminal at Newport News, the small isolated yard in Norfolk, the marine operations here, and the Peninsula Subdivision from this point to Richmond.

The C&O's mainline from Richmond to Newport News was not opened until 1881, almost a decade after the C&O's mainline had reached the Ohio in the west. At the beginning, the aim of the Virginia Central and then the C&O was to connect river navigation at Richmond with the river navigation on the Ohio/Mississippi system, which was accomplished when the C&O mainline was completed to Huntington, West Virginia, in 1873. By 1881 C&O had acquired through connections to Lexington and Louisville, Kentucky, and to Cincinnati on other railroads controlled by C&O's owner, Collis P. Huntington.

Huntington, who took over and created the C&O in 1869, and controlled its interests for the next twenty years, had visited Hampton Roads harbor as a boy and realized its potential as a railroad terminal connection with ocean-going shipping. As C&O's coal business began to expand, he realized that much of it was destined to the northeastern U. S., and that there was a growing market there, however there was no efficient route to get it there. If it were shipped by barge or ship from Newport News, it could be delivered to New York, Boston, and other places at a price very competitive with coal bought in from Pennsylvania and other regions on an all-rail route. Huntington also wanted to engage in ocean shipping to and from Europe, and in fact in the 1880s-1890s operated the C&O Steamship Company, which carried goods between Newport News and Liverpool.

Newport News was an ideal location with a huge harbor that was ice-free year-round, and at a latitude that would make export-import from across the Atlantic and to South America efficient.

After C&O's completion to the Ohio, it suffered through a period of insolvency and bankruptcy, emerging from these troubles in 1878. Though a survey of a line from Richmond to Newport News was made in 1871, nothing could be done because of the financial climate. However, by 1880, with the company back on its feet and coal business starting to become valuable, the line was built. The original 1871 surveys had been run from Richmond to five possible terminal points: Norfolk, Newport News, West Point, Yorktown, and a point on the Piankatank River. In 1872 the Newport News route was chosen.

Known as the "Peninsula Extension," it later became known on the C&O as the Peninsula Subdivision.

In March 1880 the General Assembly of Virginia authorized the construction of the new railway line, and a new survey, retracing the earlier one, was made. Construction of the line began in February 1881. The land was essentially flat and no outcrops of rock or other engineering impediments were encountered, so the work was quickly finished. An impetus to early completion was to provide a line to carry people and from the big celebration of the centennial of the Yorktown surrender, which was to occur October 18-20, 1881. The C&O's line didn't go through Yorktown, but a 4-mile extension was built to that point from Lee Hall station, to accommodate travel to the celebration. The full line was completed about that time as well, with the first work train over the road on October 16th. The Yorktown celebration had its trains, but soon afterward the branch was abandoned.

By November the line was fully operational, and C&O passenger trains began running east of Richmond for the first time. Since the inauguration of this new line was part of C. P. Huntington's grand scheme for a "true" transcontinental railroad from coast-to-coast under his leadership, he was quick to announce that through cars would operate from Louisville and Cincinnati without change to Newport News, with a Memphis-Newport News line being started shortly thereafter. Huntington eventually assembled a group of railroads in which he had controlling interest that ran from California to Virginia, linking the two oceans, but it lasted only a couple of years 1887-89. The C&O portion of it, along with some lines in Kentucky, was called the "Newport News & Mississippi Valley Company." The actual trough daily passenger operations on the Peninsula began on a daily basis May 1, 1882.

Newport News was transformed from a tiny village of a few houses into a bustling railroad terminal and port. A church, hotel, and other businesses began operation. A pier to connect with boats and ships was built, as well as a small yard of a few tracks and a turntable. Today the Newport news area is one of the largest metropolitan regions in Virginia.

Not content with the terminal at Newport News, a further extension of about 12 miles was laid from that point to Fort Monroe, the U. S. Army's famous fortress, and location of the "Hygeia," a resort-style hotel on the shoreline nearby. [The Hygeia was succeeded by the Chamberlain, which generated much

C&O passenger traffic.] The line, serving the towns of Hampton and Phoebus was opened in 1882. The final mile of track from Phoebus to Ft. Monroe was laid in 1889. Although often called the "Hampton Branch," right up to recent times, it was in fact made the eastern-most trackage of C&O's main line, and when the new milepost numbering system was adopted, Milepost "0" was installed at Ft. Monroe station, on the military post. From 1889 onward all milepost distances were measured as a distance from Fort Monroe.

At Newport News, the first coal was loaded in August 1882 into the schooner *William H. Kenzel* for delivery to New York, and a few days the new C&O collier *Kanawha* was loaded. In 1882 C&O transshipped 105,573 tons of coal at its pier. This opened a flow of coal that has extended to the present day, though the facilities: piers, yards, dumpers, etc. have been extended, built, expanded, and rebuilt over the years, the same basic pattern still operates. Coal comes in from C&O lines in West Virginia and Kentucky, is dumped into ships at Newport News,

and then goes either to the northeast, or in more recent decades, is exported around the world. The record tonnage shipped through Newport News occurred in 1957, when 23,324,115 tons was dumped.

Merchandise also became an important traffic through the port, and manifest freight trains delivered traffic for export all over the world. Incoming goods received here were shipped westward over the C&O to points along its line and connections.

It should be noted here that in the 1880s the Norfolk & Western Railway completed its coal piers at Norfolk, located across the waters of the harbor, and engaged in operations that were essentially identical to the C&O, making the Hampton Roads harbor the world's largest coal port. In 1909 the Virginian Railway added to coal shipping at Hampton Roads when its pier in Norfolk was installed.

At an early date in 1880s, C&O began serving the city of Norfolk by instituting ferry service across the

This C&O official track chart shows the layout of Brooke Avenue yard in Norfolk. C&O built its Brooke Avenue yard so as to serve the trade of that important city. It was accessed only by car float across Hampton Roads harbor. The small facility consisted of a freight station, an "Ocean Pier" which was also called "Southgate Terminal;" a passenger station for the steamers which connected with C&O trains at Newport News; a large Molasses storage tank; and several yard tracks to shift the cars that were brought in by car float.

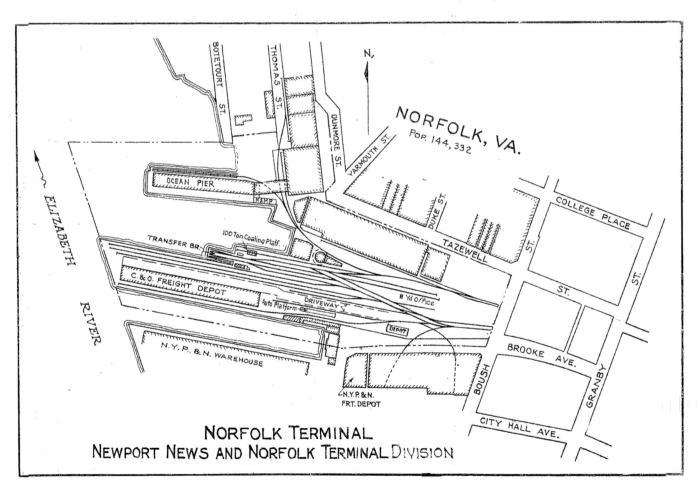

NORFOLK TERMINAL
NEWPORT NEWS AND NORFOLK TERMINAL DIVISION

harbor. This evolved into a regular passenger steamer which connected with all C&O passenger trains, and brought passengers from Norfolk to board westbound trains at Newport News, and delivered passengers for Norfolk to the ferry which carried them the last leg of their trip to Norfolk. This helped C&O compete with N&W for Norfolk-Cincinnati trade, since both lines ran in virtual parallel between those two points.

C&O also built a small yard at Brooke Avenue in Norfolk, to serve that fairly large city directly. To get its cars to and from this isolated yard, it used car floats, which were simply barges onto which the freight cars were rolled. The car float was then shepherded across the harbor by tug boats to Brooke Avenue where the cars were rolled off, and the freight delivered within the city, with the opposite for outbound freight. The little yard didn't connect with any other railroads in the city, and was served by a small switcher, usually an 0-6-0 through the steam era, and a single tiny center-cab 44-ton switcher up to the end. The passenger ferries docked at a passenger pier here. In the 1920s a big "Ocean Terminal" warehouse was built right beside the yard. One of the unusual facilities was what appeared to be a huge water tank. But it wasn't. It was for storing molasses prior to shipment. The car floats continued in operation until this facility was discontinued entirely in the early 1980s.

C&O had a large marine department headquartered at Newport News. In addition to the passenger steamer and the many car floats, there were also barges that trans-loaded break-bulk cargos to and from ships lying in the harbor. A large fleet of tug boats began operation in the mid-1880s and continued into the 1980s.

At Newport News C&O built a large wood frame passenger station in Queen Anne style architecture which served until 1942 when it was replaced by a smaller brick structure. Attached to the station was a long covered pier where the trains originated and terminated. The passenger ferries came alongside this pier and passengers transferred to and from Norfolk. The 1942 building is used as a restaurant today.

Over the years C&O continued to enlarge and upgrade its coal and merchandise piers, and installed an ore pier mainly for incoming iron ore from overseas.

An offshoot of C&O's presence in Newport News was that C. P. Huntington incorporated the Newport News Shipbuilding and Dry Dock Company. Although not connected with the C&O in any way, except through Huntington the man, it prospered in the ship building trade, and is today one of the largest industries in the state. It builds the U. S. Navy's aircraft carriers and many other naval vessels. It is the main industry at Newport News today.

Starting in World War I, the area between Williamsburg and Newport News became the location of numerous military and naval activities, and government tracks connected with the C&O at Newport News, Oyster Point, Oriana, Lee Hall (two) and Penniman. This reached a high point in WWII and has declined since then.

As C&O expanded its operations, new yards became necessary, and by the mid-20th century the huge yards at Newport News were the largest on the C&O (except Russell). One of the reasons for the large yards was the manner which coal was

C&O operated the Brooke Avenue yard with a single 0-6-0 in the steam era. Here No. 129, the regular engine, pauses between jobs on Aug. 28, 1948, with the monstrous molasses storage tank in the background. On weekends it was taken to Newport News on a car float and serviced at the engine house there. It was one of few C&O locomotives light enough to be carried on the float. - It came to C&O in 1930 with the Hocking Valley merger, having been built in 1907. (D. Wallace Johnson Photo)

A GE 44-ton center-cab 400-hp diesel replaced the little 0-6-0. It came to C&O when the Manistee & Northeastern was merged in 1955. It is not clear if the steamer remained until it arrived, or some other engine was used in the interim. It was given C&O No. 1, but was renumbered to 8303 and given the "Big C&O" simplified paint scheme in about 1967. It was retired and sold in 1974. In this 1974 scene it is at the Newport News engine terminal for its weekend servicing. (T. W. Dixon, Jr. Photo)

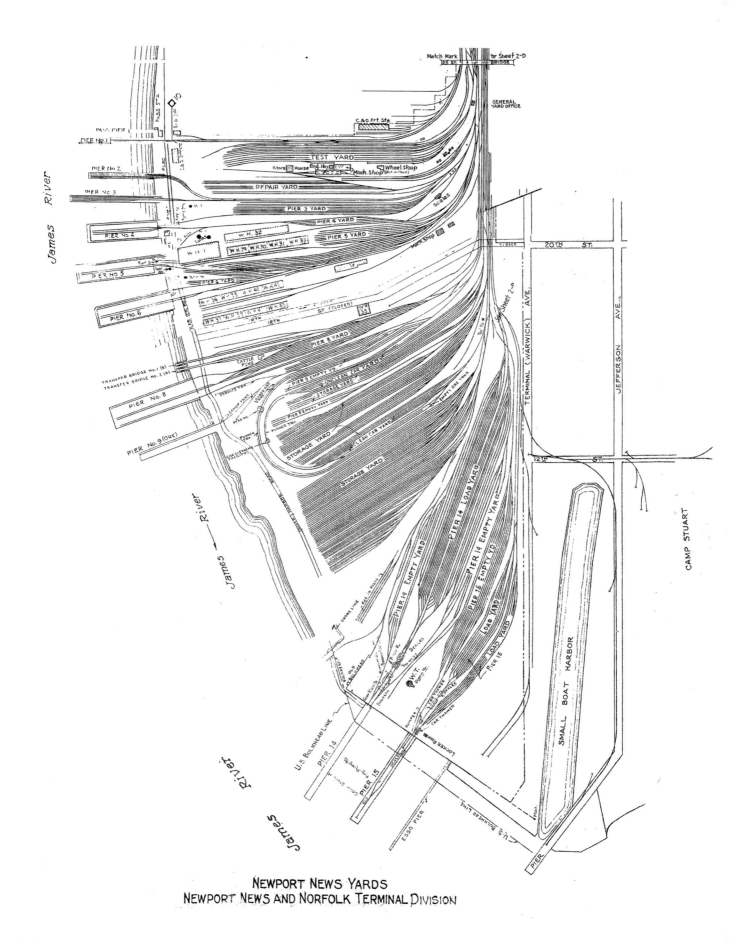

NEWPORT NEWS YARDS
NEWPORT NEWS AND NORFOLK TERMINAL DIVISION

The Newport News terminal is represented by this track chart which shows the tracks that led up to the merchandise, ore, and coal piers.

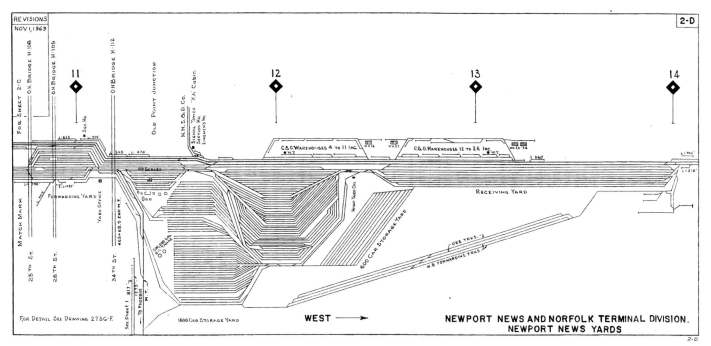

This map shows the large storage yard which was located farther back from the water. In this yard cars were received, arranged, and held until needed for dumping into particular ships.

shipped. It was purchased from various mines, and then consolidated at Newport News to await arrival of certain ships to which it was consigned. By doing this, a large yard capacity was needed to assemble the loads coming from various mines at various times. When the ship to which the coal was consigned arrived, the various loads were dumped, and then the empty cars could be returned to the miens.

After C&O decided to stop the coal dumping operations in the early 1980s, two private companies took over the work. They dump the coal on the ground and then covey it to ships as they arrive. Since the storage does not entail the use of railroad cars, the turnaround times for cars today is much faster than it was under the old system.

Once the Peninsula Subdivision was built, passenger trains began operating through Richmond to terminate here. Then in 1889 C&O acquired trackage rights over what was later the Southern Railway, the main passenger operations shifted to operate east of Charlottesville to Washington with through cars to New York. To accommodate the old line down the Piedmont to Richmond and on to Newport News, through cars were added and taken out of trains at Charlottesville. Therefore a car coming from the west on a C&O Cincinnati-Washington train would be shifted out at Charlottesville and put into a new train. This train would then carry the passengers from points west on to Richmond-Newport News-Norfolk, without their having to change trains.

Westbound the opposite occurred. This pattern lasted until the end of C&O passenger service in 1971.

As coal business grew, the single track Peninsula line was double tracked, and given modern signaling. It became a "conveyor belt" for coal moving east and empty trains moving west, interspersed with frequent passenger trains, regular manifest freights, and a couple of local freights.

The population along the 85-mile line was fairly sparse, with only Williamsburg as a point of any importance. It became more prominent after the early 1930s restoration of "Colonial Williamsburg" and figured heavily in C&O passenger advertising and interest in the 1930s-1960s.

Lee Hall was the station serving Camp Eustis (today's Fort Eustis), an important army installation in World War I, which grew in importance in WWII and after. The U. S. Military Railroad serving Ft. Eustis connected with C&O at Lee Hall.

During World War I the line saw huge traffic as men and materiel ware shipped to Europe through Newport News. In World War II this was even larger, as the Norfolk and Newport News facilities were put under coordination of the military's "Hampton Roads Port of Embarkation." The invasion of North Africa was staged from this point, and massive amounts of materiel and large movements of troops passed through the C&O's facilities throughout the war.

In the 1970s, during C&O's rationalization of its lines, part of the double track was taken up, so today the CSX Peninsula Subdivision is a single track railroad with long stretches of double track.

Today CSX still carries a large amount of coal which is delivered to the two commercial coal terminals for export shipment. Amtrak operates several trains to and from Newport News as an extension of its Northeast Corridor traffic, via Richmond. The new Amtrak depot is located at the site of the C&O's Hampton Roads Transfer station, where buses from Ft. Monroe, Hampton and Phoebus met the C&O trains after 1957.

The cross-harbor steam ferries were eliminated in 1950 and buses connected with Norfolk until 1971 when Amtrak took over.

At the western end of the line is Fulton yard. It was the location at which coal trains from the west were arranged for delivery to Newport News. Because the yard was built on a 0.63% eastward grade, it was always necessary to add helper locomotives to get the heavy trans started and up the grade. The pushers and double-headers cut off about seven miles to the east at a station called Fort Lee, and the trains were then able to proceed east without further assistance.

In the steam era C&O used its standard freight power in the form of 2-8-0s up into the 1915 era, when some of the new 2-6-6-2s began to be used on the heavy coal trains. The 2-8-2 Mikados were also common power on the line after the early-1920s. Passenger trains usually had 4-6-2s in the post-1920s era, and in the late 1940s often rated a heavy 4-6-4 Hudson type. At the end of steam in the 1945-1952 era 4-8-4 Greenbriers were also sometimes used on the line, running through east of Charlottesville. Giant T-1 2-10-4s and H-7 2-8-8-2 were used briefly on coal trains 1948-1952. With the advent of diesels, the ubiquitous GP7s and GP9s were prevalent until bigger, second, and now third generation units arrived. Today CSX powers its large coal trains using modern GE and EMD high-horsepower units.

Statistics (as of 1948):

32 named station locations plus 5 on the Hampton Branch.

Mileage 84.7 (measured from Ft. Monroe on Hampton Branch)

The Peninsula Subdivision began at Newport News (Milepost 14). The Norfolk and Newport News Terminal Division operated the trackage in Norfolk at Brooke Avenue, the terminal facilities and years, and the Hampton Branch, with its own superintendent and staff headquartered in a large yellow-brick building near the passenger station.

There were no C&O–operated branches, but several government-operated military/navel branches connected. The line had no connections to other railroads.

It is April 9, 1950, and J-3A No. 614 has a westbound passenger train at the Phoebus station. C&O ended here, at MP 1, because a hurricane had washed out the final mile to Ft. Monroe in the 1930s. This whole convoluted operation was eliminated in 1957 when buses replaced the trains. From that date onward trains originated at Newport News and were met with buses at Hampton Roads Transfer, a new platform installed at Old Point Junction. The buses accommodated passengers to Hampton, Phoebus, and Ft. Monroe. (H. Reid Photo)

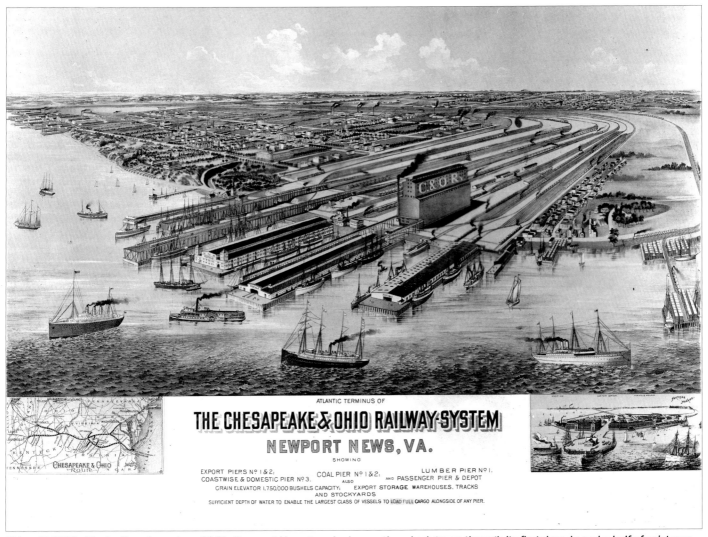

This mid-1890s illustration shows how C&O's Newport News terminal operations had grown through its first decade and a half of existence. The passenger pier is at the left, then two high-level coal piers, and three covered merchandise piers. The large structure at center is a grain elevator, which was a feature of the area until it burned in the 1920s. (TLC Collection)

This chart shows the track layout at Phoebus. Phoebus was the terminal point for C&O mainline passenger trains until 1957. They arrived from the west, called at Newport News passenger station, then backed 1.4 miles to Old Point Junction, where they turned on the wye and headed down the 14-mile "Hampton Branch" to Phoebus. Here the cars were serviced, stored in the tracks shown, then assembled to go west again, while the locomotive was backed to Old Point Junction for servicing. Trains then departed from Phoebus, went up to the junction, backed to Newport News passenger station/pier, and left to the west from that point. (C&OHS Collection)

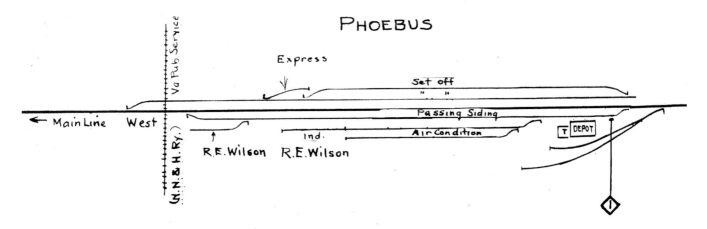

The new (1942) brick station at Newport News used the old covered passenger pier that had been built in the 1880s when the station was first sited here. Cars were parked on the pier and when the steamers came in from Portsmouth and Norfolk, passengers could be exchanged easily. The locomotive would back onto the train but would not go out on the pier. This photo was taken in the mid 1950s. (C&O Ry. Photo, C&O Hist. Soc. Coll., CSPR-3852)

The water side of the passenger pier is seen here in 1947 with the ferry parked alongside. The steamer was replaced by a bus in 1950. To the right a ship is being emptied at the ore pier. On the hill in the background is the large yellow-brick C&O terminal division office building. (C&O Ry. Photo, C&O Hist. Soc. Coll., CSPR-1190)

This car float is loaded, with general merchandise and coal traffic is en route across the harbor between Norfolk and Newport News in 1953. It had a very small engine that was used only for steering. The tug boat is supplying the power to get it across the water. (C&O Ry. Photo, C&O Hist. Soc. Coll., CSPR-3268

Another of C&O's large tug boat fleet is seen here with one of the C&O house barges which served to transfer freight to and from ships lying in the harbor ("lighters" in nautical terms). (C&O Ry. Photo, C&O Hist. Soc. Coll., CSPR-3267)

This mid-1950s aerial view shows the two coal piers (upper left) at Newport News along with the large yard where coal was stored before it was dumped. (C&O Ry. Photo, C&O Hist. Soc. Coll., CSPR-3578)

Two C&O tugs maneuver a coal ship toward the south side loader on Pier 15. In the immediate background is the import bulk materials unloading pier which has two Brownhoist gantries unloading a large ship, while the three gantries of the new import ore unloader on Pier 9 are seen in the distance. Aerial image is circa 1956-57. (C&O Ry. Photo, C&O Hist. Soc. Coll., CSPR-5078)

Pier 15's Brownhoist gantry loader is seen here as collier Lassell out of Liverpool churns up the water while docking in 1957. (C&O Ry. Photo, C&O Hist. Soc. Coll., CSPR-CL548)

Rotary dumpers at Pier 14 turn over cars and dump their contents into bunkers which then deliver it to conveyor belts. These take it out on the pier and into the four travel-ing towers that are equipped with chutes to dump it into the holds of coal ships; about 1950. (C&O Ry. Photo, C&O Hist. Soc. Coll., CSPR-2562)

This 1957 aerial view shows both Newport News coal loading piers: The recently expanded Pier 15 (left) with two ships and Pier 14 (right) with four ships. (C&O Ry. Photo, C&O Hist. Soc. Coll., CSPR-3827)

About a mile back of the piers C&O maintained a huge "Inbound" and "transit yard," seen here in 1961. Coal was purchased at mines and consigned to a particular ship, but when it arrived at Newport News that ship might not yet be there, so it had to be held until the ship arrived. This necessitated storing the coal in cars for long periods. Today this has all been eliminated because the coal is dumped on the ground in huge piles and the cars are returned very quickly, ensuring much better utilization of equip-ment. (C&O Ry. Photo, C&O Hist. Soc. Coll., CSPR-4733)

Dist. from Ft. Monroe	Tel. Calls	Station No.	Code No.	STATIONS
0.0			0001	①④**Norfolk**_____Va
			0010	City Tkt. Office
				214 Granby St.
				(Monticello Hotel)
			0011	Wharf Tkt. Office___
			0012	
			0002	①④**Porstmouth**____Va
10.0	NS	10	0016	**Newport News**__Va
			0017	④Newport News, Va., Ticket Office_____
11.3	*XA	11		Old Point Jct.____Va
1.0			0006	Phoebus_____Va
0.5			0004	{Fort Monroe_____Va
			0005	{U. S. Govt. TrackVa
2.9	HM	3	0009	①④**Hampton**_____Va
3.25				Langley Field
				Connection_____Va
11.3	*XA	11		Old Point Jct.____Va
13.7		14		N. Y. Cabin_____Va

Left and Opposite Below: These two station lists are extracted from C&O List of Stations, Agents, Officers, Etc. No. 82, August, 1948. This is the statistical compendium which will be used throughout this book. Mileposts are shown starting at Ft. Monroe. Telegraph call signs and other information is then provided for each station name

C&O also handled a large amount of other freight traffic through Newport News. One of the largest parts of this business was tobacco, seen here packed in the "hogsheads" being hoisted from merchandise pier No. 5 into a waiting ship. (C&O Ry. Photo, C&O Hist. Soc. Coll., CSPR-1432)

This long row of warehouses was located along the western edge of the C&O's Newport News facility and were used for general freight that arrived by ship or was destined to leave by ship. Note the building in the foreground, which has extensions at the bottom of its wall. This was actually protruding slanted wall to allow tobacco hogsheads to rolled up against it. (C&O Ry. Photo, C&O Hist. Soc. Coll., CSPR-5093)

C-16 class 0-8-0 switcher No. 251 is busying about its yard duties at Newport News as K-4 2-8-4 Kanawha No 2716 starts a westbound manifest freight train west about 1950. In that era C&O handled a great deal of general freight through the terminal, but this steadily declined over the decades as containerization took over, which the port was not capable of handling. (TLC Collection)

PENINSULA SUB-DIVISION

14.3		14	No. Newport News_____Va
14.6	MN	14½	0025	③Hilton Village__Va
16.5	MN	16	0028	Morrison____Va
20.3		20	0032	Oyster Point_____Va
22.7		23	0036	Oriana_____Va
				Camp Patrick
25.6		26	0040	Henry_____Va
				‡Reservoir_____Va
			0042	④Ft. Eustis_____Va
27.6	JM	28	0043	④Lee Hall_____Va
32.3		32	0050	‡Grove_____Va
34.9		35		Penniman__ ___Va
36.9	WM	37	0064	④Williamsburg____Va
40.1	CB	40	0068	Magruder (Camp Peary)_____Va
40.8		41	0069	Ewell_____Va
42.7		43	0072	Lightfoot_____Va
44.6	*UG	45	0075	Norge_____Va
47.0	AN	47	0077	Toano_____Va
51.1		51	0083	Diascund_____Va
53.4		53	0086	‡Lanexa_____Va
55.4		55	0089	Walker_____Va
58.0		58	0092	Windsor Shades__Va
61.2	FG	61	0095	Providence Forge Va
64.3		64	0099	Mountcastle_____Va
66.3		66	0102	Nance_____Va
66.9	RX	67	0103	Roxbury_____Va
71.3		72	0109	Elko_____Va
74.9		75	0112	Poplar Springs___Va
78.4		78	0115	Fort Lee_____Va
80.3		81	0118	†East Richmond__Va
80.9		81¼	0119	Twohy_____Va
81.5		81½		East End Fulton Yard_____Va
				James River_____Va
82.7			0121	①Fulton_____Va
83.2	*R	83		R. Cabin_____Va
84.4		84		②Rivanna Jct_____Va
84.7		85	0128	④Main St. Station Va
				①(Richmond)

④–Coupon Stations.
*–Day and Night Telegraph Offices.
†–No Siding.
††–Passing Siding only.
①–Junction with connecting line.
②–Junction of Sub-division shown elsewhere.
‡–Private Siding only.

The large frame station at Lee Hall, about seven miles west of the Newport News yard was the station for the U. S. Army's large Fort Eustis installation, so it saw a good deal of business. The station force is wheeling hand trucks loaded with mail over to the westbound platform to await arrival of the next train. This station has been preserved, at least in part, and moved across the tracks to private land, in the hope of a restoration (as of 2011). The Army's military railroad joined the C&O at this station as well. (C&O Ry. Photo, C&O Hist. Soc. Coll., CSPR-10393.299)

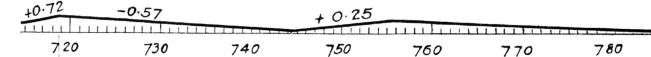

This condensed profile of the Peninsula Subdivision shows its rather low gradient. The starting grate at Fulton required helpers, and the .25% grade near Norge (near Williamsburg) sometimes required the heaviest trains to "double the hill." Otherwise the line was a dream to operate. (C&O Hist. Soc. Collection)

FULTON

FORT LEE

WILLIAMSBURG

NEWPORT NEWS

+0.72   −0.57   + 0.25

720   730   740   750   760   770   780

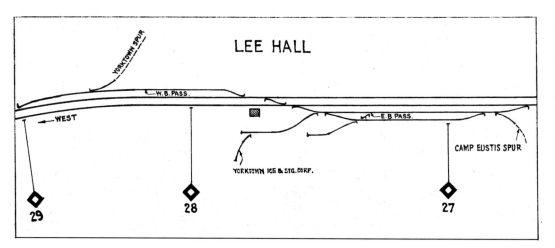

LEE HALL

YORKTOWN SPUR

W.B. PASS.

← WEST

E.B. PASS.

CAMP EUSTIS SPUR

YORKTOWN ICE & STG. CORP.

29   28   27

Track arrangement at Lee Hall shows the interchange tracks for use by the military railroad (connection show to the east), as well as a passing track, and the route of the old, long abandoned Yorktown Branch. (C&O Historical Society Collection)

The largest station on the Peninsula Subdivision was Williamsburg, where tourists to the Colonial Williamsburg restoration flocked after its completion in the 1930s. This building replaced an earlier brick structure in 1936, and still stands today serving Amtrak trains and buses. C&O heavily advertised the colonial experience at Williamsburg and Jamestown. This photo was taken in 1945. (H. Reid Photo)

K-4 2-8-4 Kanawha No. 2728 rolls a coal train east at speed as it passes the highway city limit sign for Williamsburg in November 1947. K-4s were plenty powerful to handle coal trains eastward on the Peninsula with the single exception of having to be pushed out of Fulton. (C. N. Lippencott Photo, C&O Hist. Society Collection, COHS-1713)

One of C&O's giant T-1 2-10-4 Texas types is powering a westbound empty train past the Norge depot June 11, 1952. Several of the T-1s were moved to the Peninsula in 1950 and served their last couple of years here. They were too heavy to operate west of Fulton yard because of limitations on the James River viaduct, so they rotated back and forth over the 85 miles of the Peninsula. With their uncommon power they still had to be assisted out of Fulton eastbound. The Norge station has been moved to the town library and beautifully restored on its exterior. (C&O Historical Society Collection)

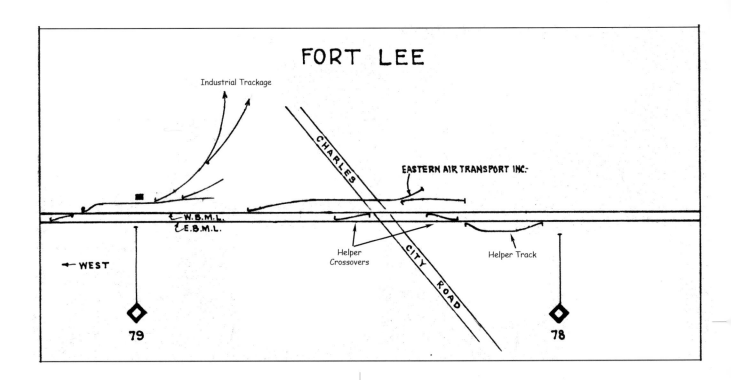

FORT LEE

Industrial Trackage

CHARLES

EASTERN AIR TRANSPORT INC.

W.B.M.L.
E.B.M.L.

CITY ROAD

← WEST

Helper
Crossovers

Helper Track

79

78

This track layout shows the arrangement at Fort Lee, which is the location where the helpers from Fulton cut off eastbound trains. The helper track and crossovers were for use by double-heading locomotives in order to return to Fulton. The pushers on the rear simply cut off and backed directly to the yard. The location was named for a Civil War emplacement, not be confused with the Army's large Ft. Lee installation at Petersburg. (C&OHS Collection)

T-1 No. 3004 rolls an eastbound coal train past the Providence Forge depot in July 1952, about at the end of steam on this subdivision. Note the hopper car at left with a conveyor for unloading. (J. I. Kelly Photo, C&O Hist. Soc. Coll., COHS-212)

C&O E8 No. 4012 leads Train 42, the Virginia section of The George Washington, *east at Norge on December 10, 1952. (C&O Historical Society Collection, COHS-1420)*

Power unlimited! Two T-1 2-10-4s pull a coal train up the grade out of Fulton yard Sept. 30, 1951, but, in fact, there was yet a third T-1 on the rear! (D. Wallace Johnson Collection)

2: Richmond

This chapter explains how the C&O served the city of Richmond and made connections at that point with other major railroads: Richmond, Fredericksburg & Potomac (RF&P), Seaboard Air Line (SAL), Atlantic Coast Line (ACL), and Southern (SR).

Richmond was the first goal and objective of the Louisa Railroad when it was conceived in 1836. The idea was to get farm products to market in Richmond. To do this the Louisa Railroad built a line to Doswell and let the RF&P take its traffic into city from that point. When the Louisa became interested in creating a much larger system and building to the west, it wanted its own line into Richmond, and after a large court battle with the RF&P, built across that line at Doswell and on into Richmond, terminating around 17th St. and Broad Street.

The Virginia Central, as Louisa became in 1850, thereafter looked on Richmond as it seat and principal base. During the War Between the States, the Virginia Central was a key line in supplying the city from the agricultural richness of the Shenandoah Valley, and with iron ore and pig iron from the western reaches of the Alleghany highlands. After the war, with Gen. Williams C. Wickham as the general manger of the C&O under C.P. Huntington's presidency, his base was at Richmond, and C&O placed many of its general offices in the city. When the Richmond Locomotive Works was establish in 1887,

and after it became a part of American Locomotive Company in 1901 until it closed in 1926, C&O was a consistent customer, preferring to buy as many of its locomotives as possible from a local supplier.

When M. E. Ingalls became president in 1889, he moved all the executive offices to Cincinnati where he was headquartered. He was at the time also president of the Big Four (Cleveland, Cincinnati, Chicago & St. Louis). It was not until 1900 that the executive and general offices were moved back to Richmond. When the Van Sweringen brothers financiers took control of the C&O in 1923, they eventually moved parts of its executive and general offices to Cleveland, though the C&O president was usually shown in the Annual Reports as having an office both in Richmond and in Cleveland. It was in the 1940s that the president, several vice- presidents and other principal offices were moved to Cleveland's Terminal Tower, leaving Richmond with most of the operating personnel. The mechanical and engineering departments moved to Huntington, W.Va. in about 1960, and with the C&O/B&O consolidation of the mid-to-late-1960s, many other offices moved to Baltimore, leaving Richmond devoid of executive and managerial C&O offices.

However, Richmond was important to the C&O quite aside from its headquarters offices. It was a large city with much commerce and manufacturing so it needed a good deal of raw materials and shipped

Looking toward Richmond from the west, the Rivanna Subdivision tracks are in the center, winding along the old James River & Kanawha Canal. The James River viaduct is in the river, along the left back in the center as it heads toward Fulton yard, out of the photo to the right. This photo was taken in 1958. (C&O Ry. Photo, C&O Historical Society Collection, CSPR-3999)

James River Viaduct

To Fulton Yard

2nd Street Yard area

Old JR&K Canal

Rivanna Subdivision racks arriving from Clifton Forge

a good traffic in finished products. It was also a point to which connections to the southeast could be made on the main lines of the SAL and ACL, and on a a secondary line of the SR. To the north, the RF&P was 1/5th owned by C&O and supplied it with connections from the north as needed, but this connection was not as important since C&O connected with RF&P's Potomac Yard via trackage rights over the SR main line between Orange and Alexandria.

C&O had several routes radiating from Richmond. First, the old original C&O mainline, the Piedmont Subdivision, ran from Fulton yard on the eastern fringe of the city through Main Street station and 17th Street Yard northwestward to Gordonsville and Charlottesville. Second, the Rivanna Subdivision ran along the James River westward from a point near Main Street Station to Gladstone, thence to Clifton Forge. Finally, the Peninsula Subdivision began at Fulton yard and ran to Newport News.

Within Richmond C&O had several yards. Probably the oldest was 17th Street Yard on the Piedmont line, which by the mid 20th-Century had become mainly a passenger car repair shop area. Second Street Yard was located on the western fringe of the city along the James River and was the point at which the old Richmond & Alleghany had arrived in the city. It was retained by C&O on its Rivanna Subdivision, but was a very small operation, used mainly as a switching base for local industries.

The largest of C&O yards was Fulton, located on the eastern fringe. It was here that coal and manifest freight arriving for forwarding to Newport News was staged. Ninth Street yard was strictly for use for inbound freight and was the location of C&O's inbound

freight station (handling LCL freight and team tracks). The outbound freight station with attendant tracks and team track area was located beside the Main Street Station complex, just west of the station.

Connecting all of this like a spine was the James River Viaduct. It ran from a point on the Rivanna Subdivision past Main Street Station, and on to Fulton Yard, lying in the bed of the James River on its northern bank. Before it was built in 1900-02, C&O trains arriving either by the James River or Piedmont lines had to work through city traffic and Church Hill Tunnel under a portion of the city, to get east of the city. Fulton yard, the viaduct and Main Street Station were all installed at the turn of the 20th Century to alleviate the bottleneck and to expedite traffic that was growing and was expected to expand by many fold, which it did.

Main Street Station itself has a large French Renaissance style head-house with a train shed to its rear. The shed had tracks running beside it and several stub end tracks under it. On the eastern side C&O trains operating on the Piedmont Subdivision used it as the stop for mainline name trains, and the James River Line local accommodation trains came into this side of the station by using the half wye at Rivanna Junction, on the viaduct. On the west side of the station the Seaboard Air Line Railroad's main Richmond-Florida line was used by all its high class Florida service and other passenger trains. Richmond's other two largest passenger carriers, ACL and RF&P, built the great Broad Street Station out to the northwestern side of the city in 1917. SAL moved its trains there in 1959. Southern had its own station for its branch line passenger trains serving Richmond as well. C&O passen-

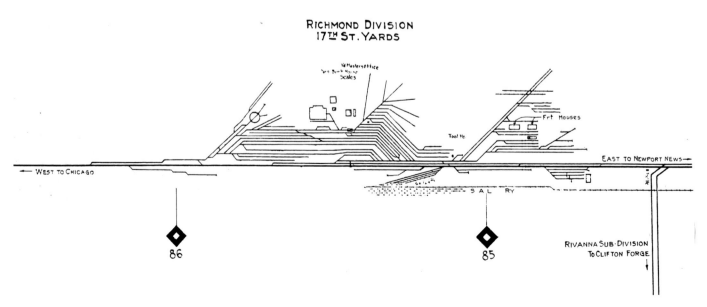

RICHMOND DIVISION
17TH ST. YARDS

ger trains continued here until Amtrak day in 1971. Amtrak continued the station until 1975 when it was closed. After a disastrous fire it was rebuilt and rehabilitated and a shopping mall was put under the train shed. After the mall failed, the building was then used for Virginia state offices. It is now being used again by Amtrak for its trains using the Washington-Richmond-Newport News segment of its system.

The triple crossing was one of Richmond's famous railroad sights. Near Main Street the C&O crossed over the SAL, which in turn crossed over the Southern's West Point line, one on top of the other. Postcards began showing this in the 1908 period, with a C&O train on top, SAL in the middle and SR beneath, always posed.

Another interesting historical footnote about the C&O in Richmond is the buried train in Church Hill Tunnel. It was in 1925 that a work train and crew was in the old tunnel (built 1872 to give C&O access to the docks) when it collapsed burying the train and several men. The train is still there, locomotive, cars and all.

Today only Fulton yard is still in use, still staging coal trains to Newport News and empties west. The Piedmont Subdivision is leased to the Buckingham Branch Railroad, and the other facilities have been abandoned and sold off for other development.

A small water tank and a few remaining buildings as well as a couple of tracks were all that was left of 2nd Street Yard, near the end of the Rivanna Subdivision line, when this photo was taken in 1972. (T. W. Dixon, Jr. Photo, C&O Historical Society Collection, COHS-28998)

The principal work of the C&O in Richmond was the long James River viaduct which connected its various lines and yards, and by elevating the tracks avoided he city's congestion. Here, in 1959, a set of the short-lived RDC cars are crossing the viaduct en route between Gordonsville and Charlottesville where they were used as a connection for the Washington-Cincinnati trains. (C&O Ry. Photo, C&O Historical Society Collection, CSPR-10787.05)

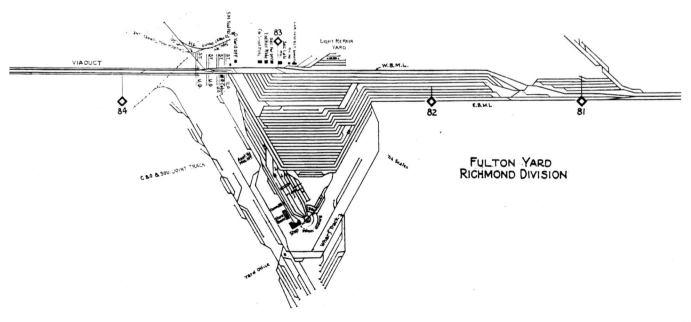

FULTON YARD
RICHMOND DIVISION

Main Street Station, looking down toward the train shed. The tracks to the left are the Piedmont Subdivision coming in from Gordonsville and curving left out of the station toward Fulton Yard. The tracks on the right are the Seaboard Air Line main line from Florida. JN Cabin, the tower in the center, regulated movements through the station including the sub-end tracks under the canopy. To the left are C&O team tracks associated with the outbound freight station. To the right is SAL's LCL freight station. In the distance the clock tower of the station's head-house is the landmark. The white concrete piers beyond the station are Interstate 95 being built in this ca. 1959 photo. (C&O Historical Society Collection, COHS-29062)

E8 4023 is in charge of a seven-car train eastbound out of the station, headed to Newport News in about 1958. This was the typical composition of Virginia sections of the name trains, operating between Charlottesville and Newport News, and serving Richmond as a main stop. The French Renaissance style of the head house with its distinctive clock tower is prominent in this photo. (C&O Ry. Photo, C&O Historical Society Collection, CSPR-4367)

Passengers in the main waiting room area of Main Street station in 1946, which was located on the second floor, next to the elevated tracks. They could be waiting for a C&O train or for an SAL train. The windows open to the street side of the building, while the train shed is to the photographer's back. (TLC Collection)

In this early 1950s photo a renovated waiting room is well filed with passengers. The former news stand was converted to a ticket selling area. In the earlier years the tickets were sold in the downstairs lobby. (C&O Ry. Photo, C&O Historical Society Collection, CSPR-11662.01)

GP7 No 5862 switches passenger cars under the Main Street Station train shed July 28, 1965. Normally C&O trains used the tracks in the left foreground, on the east side of the station unless they had cars that terminated or originated at Richmond. In this case a special train is being made up. (C&O Historical Society Collection)

This aerial view shows the junction point of the Rivanna and Piedmont Subdivisions at Rivanna Junction. (C&O Historical Society Collection, COHS-29060)

On June 22, 1951, C&O J-3a 4-8-4 Greenbrier No. 610 brings the Virginia section of an eastbound train over the James River viaduct about to enter Fulton yard with a combination of new lightweight cars and older heavyweights still in green. (D. Wallace Johnson photo)

Just to the west of Main Street Station the Piedmont Subdivision tracks passed through 17th Street yard and on toward Gordonsville and Charlottesville, passing the old site of Richmond Locomotive Works. (TLC Collection)

Site of former Richmond Locomotive Works / ALCO-Richmond Plant

To Charlottesville

17th Street Yard

To Main Street Station

The triple crossing became a subject of interest at an early date. It was created when C&O built its James River viaduct and SAL's line was elevated through Main Street Station ca. 1902. C&O's Rivanna Subdivision is on the top, and in this 1950 photo has a K-3a with an empty coal train headed west. In the middle a SAL train is pointed south, and beneath is a Southern local is on it's West Point branch. (C&O Ry. Photo, C&O Historical Society Collection, CSPR-29007)

The main C&O yard in Richmond was Fulton. Here coal trains were staged for dispatched to Newport News. The roundhouse shows three stages of expansion through the years. The 800-ton coaling station was exactly the same as the ones at Hinton, W. Va. and Stevens, Ky. The yard was built on a curve and more importantly on an eastbound grade of 0.57%,wich increased to 0.63% east of the yard. (C&O Ry. Photo, C&O Historical Society Collection, CSPR-3573)

C-15 0-8-0 No. 116 and T-1 2-10-4 No. 3022 are pushing coal Extra 3032 east out of Fulton yard on September 9, 1951 at Darbytown Road. Because Fulton was built on an eastward grade all coal trains had to be assisted out of the yard to Fort Lee, a distance of 4.3 miles. (D. Wallace Johnson Collection)

3: The Piedmont Subdivision

The next area of the C&O to be covered is the Piedmont Subdivision, running almost a hundred miles, between Richmond and Charlottesville. This stretch of line is the oldest part of the C&O system, having been originally the Louisa Railroad. It was here that the first predecessor of the C&O began its operations.

By the 1830s railroads were being incorporated and projected in many states, and Virginia's populace was interested as well. The Baltimore & Ohio had proven the efficacy of railroad transportation using a carriage with steel wheels rolling on a set of steel or iron rails, and powered by a steam engine designed into a locomotive. In Virginia there was an early railroad movement, and in the decades 1830-1850 numerous lines were projected and built, both east-west and north-south through the Commonwealth.

People interested in improving transportation in the region met at Louisa Court House in the fall of 1835 and obtained a charter from the General Assembly on February 18, 1836, to sell stock in a new company to be called the Louisa Railroad. The Commonwealth of Virginia subscribed part of the stock and appointed two of the five directors of the road. After money was raised, the line was built between Taylorsville and Frederick's Hall under the leadership of the line's first President, Frederick Harris of Frederick's Hall. Construction was by C. R. Mason, who would be the construction engineer of many future works of the railroad, through the westward construction of the C&O in the 1870s. The line was opened in December 1837 with trains starting on the Richmond, Fredericksburg & Potomac (RF&P) in Richmond, and going through to the junction at what is now Doswell, then on to Frederick's Hall. By December 1838 the additional 12 miles to Louisa Court House was opened. The original aim of the line was to operate a far a Gordonsville, and in 1840 the road was opened to that point.

At the beginning of operations the Louisa Railroad Company did not buy its own equipment, but leased out its operation to the already well-established RF&P, so the company's efforts were concentrated on expanding its line. This continued until the contract was abrogated in 1847 and the Louisa began operating its own line with its own equipment.

The Louisa projected its line to Charlottesville and westward from there as early as 1841, but funds and local interest were lacking. By 1850 the funds had become available and the line was extended to Charlottesville. At the same time Louisa wanted to build into Richmond since it no longer had access to the city over the RF&P, but the RF&P interposed legal objections, and it was not until 1851 that the road was extended from Doswell into Richmond.

Piedmont Subdivision station list as of 1948. Of these 19 had full time agents.

PIEDMONT SUB-DIVISION

Dist. from Ft. Monroe	Tel. Calls	Station No.	Code No.	STATIONS
			0125	①②④**Richmond**___Va
83.2		83		R. Cabin._____
84.7	*JN	85		J. N. Cabin._____
84.7	*DO	85		Dispatcher's Office__
84.7		85	0128	Main St. Station.____
			0130	Baggage._____
				⎧Broad St. Station___
				⎩9th St. Station._____
			0129	④City Tkt. Office,
				706 E. Grace St.___
			0127	Salvage Ware-
				house._____Va
85.4				Richmond Shops_Va
85.7				A. R. Cabin._____Va
87.9		88	0130	Highland Park___Va
88.6		89	0132	Atlantic Rural Expo-
				sition Depot____Va
90.1		90	0134	†Chickahominy___Va
91.3		91	0136	Ellerson_____Va
94.5		93	1040	Atlee._____Va
97.0		97	0146	†Ashcake_____Va
99.2		99	0149	Peake._____Va
101.1		101	0151	†Cady._____Va
102.7	HA	103	0154	Hanover_____Va
105.4		105	0158	†Wickham_____Va
107.3		107	0161	††South Anna_____Va
111.8	*HN	112	0168	①Doswell_____Va
114.7		115	0172	Verdon_____Va
115.9		116	0173	†North Anna_____Va
117.6		118	0178	††Noel_____Va
119.7		120	0181	Hewlett_____Va
121.6		122	0184	†Holliday_____Va
122.8		123	0186	Teman._____Va
124.4	BD	124	0188	Beaver Dam_____Va
127.2		127	0191	Tyler_____Va
129.4		129	0193	Bumpass_____Va
131.3		131	0195	Buckner_____Va
134.6	FH	135	0198	Frederick Hall__Va
139.4		139	0201	Pendleton_____Va
140.7	SV	141	0204	④Mineral_____Va
146.5	CU	147	0215	④Louisa_____Va
147.2		148	0216	Bibb._____Va
151.0	ON	151	0219	Trevilian_____Va
154.2		154	0222	Green Spring_____Va
157.1		157	0225	Melton_____Va
160.4	*G	160	0228	②④Gordonsville__Va
165.2	*DA	165	0250	②Lindsay_____Va
167.4		167	0285	④Cobham_____Va
170.3		170	0288	Campbell_____Va
172.0		172	0290	†Rugby_____Va
174.1	K	174	0292	④Keswick_____Va
176.3		176	0295	Shadwell_____Va
181.4	*MO	181	0301	①④Charlottesville_Va

†-No Siding.
††-Passing Siding only.
④-Coupon Stations.
*-Day and Night Telegraph Offices.
①-Junction with connecting lines.
②-Junction of Sub-division shown elsewhere.

With its expanded mission, the Louisa changed its name to Virginia Central in 1850, and began the process of building westward across the Blue Ridge and to the foot of the Alleghany mountains, where it was to connect with a state-sponsored line called the Covington & Ohio. The Covington & Ohio in turn was to built across the trans-Alleghany region to the Ohio.

Thus, by 1850 the new Virginia Central comprised what would later be the Piedmont Subdivision of the C&O. Since it was built in a region that had few mineral resources, its commerce in the early period was primarily agricultural traffic and passengers. Over the decades, as the C&O built westward and its traffic grew, the Piedmont Subdivision remained a rural agricultural line, that would eventually be most important for handling C&O's through passenger and freight trains between Charlottesville and Richmond.

There was some development of mineral traffic when branches were opened out of Mineral which carried the mineral products. The 1.76 mile Arminius Mines Branch was built in 1885 by the Arminius Copper Mines Company, and was operated under lease by the C&O from 1906 until it was abandoned with the closing of the mine in 1927. The other branch from Mineral was also built 3.77 miles by the Sulphur Mines Company in 1885 and operated by C&O under lease until December 31, 1925. Other than this, some rock quarries gave the C&O a little business, but little else except farm production was available in local business.

There were no towns on the line of large population except the terminal point of Charlottesville. Gordonsville did have a good agricultural traffic base, as did the other small-town stations. However,

the traffic over the line was considerable in that it comprised the main line of the road as trains were forwarded between Charlottesville and Richmond. This increased as the coal business blossomed after the opening of the Peninsula Subdivision in 1881.

By the middle decades of the 20th Century, in which era this book's emphasis lies, the Piedmont was handling eight passenger trains per day, six of which were sections of C&O's through Washington-Cincinnati trains that were broken out and consolidated at Charlottesville. Many still had stops along the Piedmont at Gordonsville (where the line to Washington actually diverged), Louisa, and Hanover. The many smaller rural stations along the line were accommodated by a local passenger train. Of course, local freights operated in both directions. The line was not used for very much through fast freight, nor for coal, because after 1890 the coal was going by way of the James River Line (see Chapters 6–8), and the fast freight was either on this line, if it was headed for Richmond and Newport News, or going eastward to Washington from Charlottesville and traveling over only a small section of the Piedmont Subdivision.

It should be noted that, over time, the exact limits of the Piedmont Subdivision changed, sometimes stopping at Gordonsville, and sometimes at Charlottesville. In the mid-20th Century scope of this book, the Piedmont ran from Fulton Yard in Richmond, where the Peninsula Subdivision ended, through Main Street Station (near where it joined with the Rivanna Subdivision) and 17th Street Shops and yard in that city, thence to Charlottesville. After 1889 mainline passenger trains diverged eastward (northeastward geographically) at Gor-

F-15 light Pacific No. 455 takes Train No. 44 past the small shelter station at Chickahominy in June 1948. This style of "flag stop" station was standard on the C&O, most being built in the 1895-1915 era, and many lasted until the end of local trains in the mid-1950s. Even in 1948 such stations were anachronisms, but it fits perfectly with the rural nature of the Piedmont. (J. I. Kelly Photo, C&O Hist. Soc. Collection, COHJS-119)

donsville toward Washington, as did the fast freight trains headed for Potomac Yard in Alexandria, so the stretch of 21 miles between Charlottesville and Gordonsville as a very busy portion of the line.

In more modern times, as passenger service and local freight traffic declined, the Piedmont Subdivision became a backwater on the C&O and in C&O/B&O-Chessie System era it was viewed as probably non-essential. CSX leased it to the short-line Buckingham Branch Railroad in the 1990s. The line is currently operated by Buckingham Branch, along with the former C&O Mountain Subdivision. It carries Buckingham Branch's local business, plus many westbound CSX empty coal trains between Richmond and Clifton Forge.

Steam motive power on the Piedmont consisted of generally smaller engines, since it had easy grades and light overall traffic. Passenger trains between Richmond and Charlottesville, which were lighter than those on the Charlottesville-Washington line, were usually handled by 4-6-2 Pacific types. In later years of the 1940s 4-6-4 Hudsons, 4-8-2 Mountains, and occasionally 4-8-4 Greenbriers were used. Freight trains were handled almost exclusively by 2-8-2 Mikados and 2-10-2 Santa Fe types. The 2-10-2 was an unusual wheel arrangement on C&O, with its locomotives of this type having been all purchased second hand or acquired through merger. They proved to be exactly what C&O wanted for this region, with plenty of power to handle the assigned traffic. From the mid-1940s to the end of steam K-4 class 2-8-4s were also used.

When diesels arrived the ubiquitous E8 passenger diesels were used, first in pairs. Later a single unit as assigned. When Amtrak took over, the E8s were replaced by a GP9 (with steam generator) that hauled one or two cars as the connection between Charlottesville and Richmond. This short train was also soon discontinued, replaced by a motor bus connection. Later higher horsepower second and third generation diesels were used, and today CSX uses its giant EMD and GE units for the empty hopper trains, while Buckingham Branch uses a variety of second and third-hand locomotives for its local business.

Statistics (as of 1948)

Mileage: 98.2 miles

Stations: 43 (in 1948, 23 of these were staffed with an agent).

Branches connecting: None (Note: the Sulphur Mine and Atremis branches from Mineral had been abandoned.)

J-2 Mountain type No. 546 rushes Train No. 46, the Virginia section of The Sportsman *past the wooden water tank at South Anna in June 1948. 100,000 gallon wooden tanks with steel stanchions were fairly common on C&O up to the end of steam, even though many steel tanks had been erected after 1915. (J. I. Kelly Photo, C&O Hist. Society Collection, COHS-127)*

Track layout at Doswell, showing C&O and RF&P interchanges.C&O Historical Society Collection)

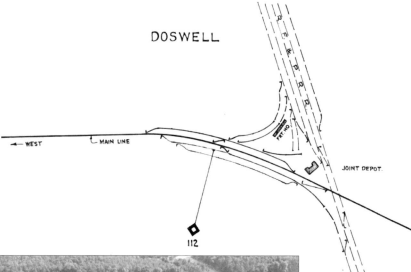

DOSWELL

JOINT DEPOT.

← WEST   MAIN LINE

112

This aerial view shows Doswell, where the north-south high speed main line of the RF&P was crossed by C&O's Piedmont Subdivision. The station arranged in the full wye was built and owned by RF&P, but was jointly operated by both railroads. The big freight station was also a joint facility. (TLC Collection)

RF&P To Richmond

To Richmond

Passenger Station

Piedmont Subdivision

To Gordonsville

Freight Station

F-16 Pacific No. 466 is on C&O Train No. 46, The Sportsman, as it pulls into the Doswell station in 1937. HN Tower at right was a joint RF&P/C&O facility, but manned by RF&P, as was the freight and passenger stations. J. I. Kelly Photo, C&O Historical Society Collection, COHS-340)

Two E8s are seen with No. 46, the Virginia section of The Sportsman, *in about 1954 as one or two passengers prepare to board or meet someone at Doswell. (S. K. Bolton Photo, TLC Collection)*

Beaverdam boasts this fine old brick depot. The original walls date from antebellum Virginia Central days. It was burned during the war by Federal raiders, but rebuilt. This 1976 photo shows that it was still manned and had an active semaphore train order signal. The station has been restored today, and is perhaps the oldest former C&O structure left. (C. J. Bocklage, Jr. Photo, C&O Hist. Society Collection)

This tiny station was at Frederick Hall, locale of the very birth of the C&O in 1836, as it looked in about 1940. The building itself was new, having replaced an older, much larger structure, which was perhaps the third station at the spot. Frederick Harris was the first president and prime mover in the Louisa Railroad. (C&O Historical Society Collection)

Louisa, another of the earliest stations on the Louisa Railroad is seen here in its last iteration in 1938. The station is of the 1890 C&O standard station design featuring the characteristic verge boards on the eaves. The building the background was the freight station. (C&O Railway Photo, C&O Historical Society Collection)

Gordonsville depot and G Cabin were set in the wye formed by the Washington Subdivision (left) and the Piedmont. The large station here was unique in design. B-1 2-10-2 No. 2951 has manifest freight No. 95, coming in from Potomac Yard on July 10, 1950. (J. I Kelly Photo, C&OHS Collection)

This view of the Gordonsville station is from the Washington Subdivision line looking west in about 1970. The station is long gone now. (T. W. Dixon, Jr. Photo, C&O Hist. Society Collection)

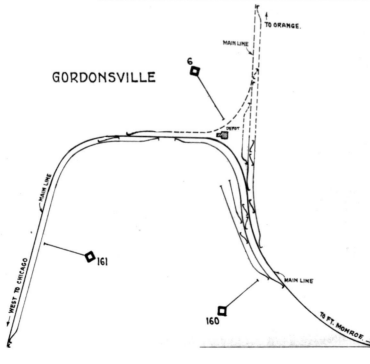

Track layout at Gordonsville showing the station sitting in the wye formed by the Washington and Piedmont Subdivisions and connecting track between the two. (C&O Historical Society Collection)

Scheduled trains, extracted from a 1947 C&O Employee timetable shows the passenger and scheduled freights on the Washington and Piedmont Subdivisions. Nos. 53 and 54 were the local freights. Nos. 94 and 97 were the only scheduled freights. Everything else was passenger. Note that this DOES include trains coming from Washington that joined the Piedmont Subdivision at Gordonsville. (TLC Collection)

RICHMOND DIVISION
WASHINGTON AND PIEDMONT SUBDIVISIONS
EASTWARD

Side Track Capacity in Cars (41 ft.)	Distance from Charlottesville	Supplement "A" to TIME TABLE No. 134. In Effect Sunday, Nov. 30, 1947. STATIONS.	6 Daily	2 Daily	42 Daily	4 Daily	46 Daily	30 Daily Ex. Sun.	44 Daily	116 Sunday Only	104 Daily	98 Daily	404 Mixed Daily Ex. Sun.	96 Daily	94 Daily	54 Daily Ex. Sun.
	114.9	Wt. WASHINGTON (EEDT)	A 4 00	8 15		12 40					8 00					
Yard	108.7	Wt Potomac Yard										10 30		1 30		
	106.7	W Alexandria	s 3 35	7 50		s12 15					s 7 35					
o114	30.2	ORANGE (WEDT)	f 1 45	6 10		s10 40					s 5 25	7 30	9 30	10 00		
p 80	29.2	South Orange														
o184	21.0	Wy GORDONSVILLE	s 1 30	5 50		10 25					s 5 08		9 05			
Yard	98.8	Wt R. Cabin													2 30	1 00
	97.1	W RICHMOND			8 30	1 15		8 00	1 00	6 30						
	95.9	Wt A. R. Cabin (WEDT)			8 22	1 07		7 50	12 54	6 25 [41]					2 16	12 30
p 71 o 12	87.4	Atlee			8 10	12 55		f 7 33	12 40	6 08					1 59	12 14 [47]
p 96 o 17	78.9	Hanover			7 58	12 44		f 7 15	12 24 [47]	f 5 50 [141]					1 42	11 50
p 65	73.7	South Anna			7 52	12 39		f 7 02	12 05	f 5 35					1 25	11 35
p 69 o 99	69.7	y Doswell			7 47 [53]	12 34 [47]		s 6 57	11 59	s 5 30					1 17	11 25
p 65	64.1	Noel			7 41	12 15		f 6 46	11 50	f 5 18					1 00	11 10
p 66 o 17	57.1	Beaver Dam			7 34	12 08		s 6 34	11 37	f 5 05					12 48	10 55
p 65 o 8	51.9	Bumpass			7 28	12 03		f 6 21	11 27	f 4 53					12 38	10 40
p 65 o 6	46.9	W Frederick Hall			7 23	11 58		s 6 13	11 20	s 4 46					12 15 [43]	10 30
p 67 o 88	40.7	Mineral			7 16	11 51		f 6 00	11 10	f 4 35					11 56	10 00 [53]
p 65 o 18	34.9	Louisa			7 10	11 45		s 5 47	11 02 [53]	f 4 24					11 43	9 35
p 65 o 6	30.4	Trevilian			7 05	11 40 [53]		f 5 38	10 54	f 4 15					11 34	9 25
o184	21.0	Wy GORDONSVILLE			6 53	11 28		s 5 13	s10 40	s 3 54					11 16 [97]	9 00
p103 o184	21.0	Wy GORDONSVILLE	s 1 30	5 50	6 53	10 25	11 28	s 5 13	s10 40	s 3 54	s 5 08		s 8 40			
p 65 o372	16.2	y Lindsay	1 24	5 44	6 45	10 19	11 22	f 5 07	10 33	s 3 48		6 45	8 30			
p 51 o 5	11.1	W Campbell	1 19	5 39	6 40	10 14	11 17	f 4 55	10 25	f 3 40						
o 7	7.3	Keswick						f 4 47	f 10 17	s 3 32						
p 65	4.0	Massie	1 10	5 30	6 31	10 05	11 08									
Yard	.0	Wt CHARLOTTESVILLE	1 05	5 25	6 25	10 00	11 03	4 30	10 05	3 20	4 40	L	8 40	10 30		7 45

RICHMOND DIVISION
WASHINGTON AND PIEDMONT SUBDIVISIONS
WESTWARD

Calls	Hours Open	Distance from R. Cabin	Distance from Washington	Supplement "A" to TIME TABLE No. 134. In Effect Sunday, Nov. 30, 1947. STATIONS.	47 Daily	5 Daily	141 Daily	41 Daily	1 Daily	43 Daily	3 Daily	103 Daily	93 Daily	403 Mixed Daily Ex. Sun.	95 Daily	97 Daily	53 Daily Ex. Sun.
H	Continuous		.0	Wt. WASHINGTON (EEDT)		11 45			6 30		11 25	12 01					
YD	Continuous		6.2	Wt Potomac Yard									4 00		00		
	Continuous		8.2	W Alexandria		s12 03				s 6 48	s11 43	s12 20					
OH	Continuous		84.7	ORANGE (WEDT)			s 1 50		8 28		1 25		f 2 15	7 30	11 20	4 50	
			85.7	South Orange													
G	Continuous		93.9	Wy GORDONSVILLE			s 2 02		8 38		s 1 36	s 2 30		11 35			
R	Continuous	.0		Wt R. Cabin												8 30	6 00
JN	Continuous	1.7		W RICHMOND	12 01			5 20	6 35	11 00					8 40		6 15
		2.9		Wt A. R. Cabin (WEDT)	12 03				6 37 [116]	11 02					8 40		6 15
		11.4		Atlee	12 14 [54]			f 5 36	6 48	11 15					8 55		6 40
HA	7.00 a. to 4.00 p. Ex. Sun.	19.9		Hanover	12 24 [44]			f 5 50 [116]	6 58	11 27					9 10		7 15 [50]
		25.1		W South Anna	12 29			f 5 56	7 03	11 33					9 18		7 25
HN	Continuous	29.1		y Doswell	12 34 [44]			f 6 03	7 08	11 40					9 27		7 47 [42]
		34.7		Noel	12 41			f 6 12	7 14	11 48					9 37		8 10
BD	6.15 a. to 3.15 p. Ex. Sun.	41.7		Beaver Dam	12 48			f 6 23	7 20	11 59					9 49		8 50
		46.9		Bumpass	12 54			f 6 33	7 25	12 06					9 59		9 00
FH	10.00 a.m. to 7.00 p.m.	51.9		W Frederick Hall	12 59			f 6 41	7 30	12 15 [94]					10 07		9 30
SV	8.30 a. to 5.30 p. Ex. Sun.	58.1		Mineral	s 1 05			f 6 51	7 36	12 26					10 18		10 00 [44]
CU	8.30 a. to 5.30 p. Ex. Sun.	63.9		Louisa	s 1 12			f 7 02	7 42	12 36					10 28		11 02 [44]
ON	7.30 a. to 4.30 p. Ex. Sun.	68.4		Trevilian	1 20			7 10	7 47	12 43					10 36		11 40 [44]
G	Continuous	77.8		Wy GORDONSVILLE	s 1 32			s 7 22	7 58	s12 55					10 53 [94]		12 01
G	Continuous	77.8	93.9	Wy GORDONSVILLE	s 1 32	s 2 02	s 7 25	7 58	8 38	s 1 00	s 1 36	s 2 30		2 10			
DA	Continuous	82.6	98.7	y Lindsay									f 2 16			5 35	
		87.7	103.8	W Campbell													
K	8.00 a.m. to 5.00 p.m.	91.5	107.6	Keswick													
		94.8	110.9	Massie	1 52	2 25	7 49	8 20	8 55	1 33	1 58	2 50					
MO	Continuous	98.8	114.9	Wt CHARLOTTESVILLE	2 05	2 37	8 00	8 30	9 05	1 45	2 10	3 05	9 30		12 25		1 00

4: The Washington Subdivision

This chapter will deal with the line of road beginning at Gordonsville and running into Washington, D.C.

The original route of the Virginia Central was from Richmond and Doswell northwesterly to Gordonsville and thence to Charlottesville, as explained in other chapters. However, in the antebellum era the Orange and Alexandria Railroad had built a line from Alexandria south to Lynchburg, which became part of the Virginia Midland and then the Richmond & Danville companies after the war. It had a line that ran from Orange to Gordonsville, and then it operated over the C&O into Charlottesville and picked up its own line southward at that point.

In 1880 a new Virginia Midland line was built between Orange and Charlottesville, thus leaving the line between Orange and Gordonsville without through traffic.

At the same time, the C&O was exploring expansion efforts, which resulted in construction of the Peninsula line in 1881, the Cincinnati Division in 1889, and acquisition of the Richmond & Alleghany (James River Line) in 1890. As early as 1879 a survey for a direct C&O line to Washington was proposed, and an actual survey from Crozet on the Mountain Subdivision into Washington was made in 1889. It was also in 1889 that M. E. Ingalls, new president of the C&O, arranged with the Virginia Midland (R&D) for trackage rights into Alexandria and over the RF&P and PRR into Washington. This avoided the necessity for C&O to build a new line and pleased the Virginia Midland because it would not have a competitor and could collect rent from C&O's use of its line. The new trackage arrangement was first and foremost to handle the new *Fast Flying Virginian* ultra-luxurious through train, so that it could then operate solid over the PRR on to New York, thus establishing it as a fully through New York-Cincinnati operation and breaking C&O into the "big time" of passenger operations.

Soon thereafter C&O began to operate other passenger trains and freights over this line as well, with a 99-year lease on the trackage between Orange and Charlottesville, and a 99-year trackage rights agreement over the Virginia Midland line to Alexandria. This opened northeastern connections to both passenger and freight traffic. When Richmond, Fredericksburg & Potomac's Potomac Yard was built in 1906 and expanded in the years following, it became C&O's eastern gateway to the great northeastern railroad network. C&O also became

part-owner of the RF&P. C&O used a very short stretch of RF&P trackage in Alexandria as well as Potomac yard. Pennsylvania, Baltimore & Ohio, and Southern were the other joint owners of the RF&P, along with the Commonwealth of Virginia.

Thus, C&O's entire Washington Subdivision was operated on trackage that was leased (Gordonsville-Orange) or by trackage rights (Orange-Alexandria and Alexandria-Washington).

In the years that followed this line was most heavily used as a passenger route, with fast freights operating into Potomac Yard as well. Local freights were also operated using the trackage rights. As passenger service declined and trains were discontinued the route became less important, and when the CSX merger occurred, it was no longer a viable route for fast freight. The manifest freight was now diverted to Richmond and up the RF&P to Potomac Yard, thus when the trackage agreement expired in 1987, it was not renewed. However, the line is still used by Buckingham Branch for freight as far as Orange, and by Amtrak's Cardinal operating along C&O's old Washington-Cincinnati routing.

Motive power in the steam era for passenger trains consisted of 4-4-0s and 4-6-0s until arrival of the Pacific type 4-6-2s in 1902. From that time forward Pacifics were regular power for most trains on the Washington Subdivision. By the 1920s and '30s the F-16, 17, 18, and 19 classes were commonly used, with F-18s and

Washington Subdivision station list 1948.

WASHINGTON SUB-DIVISION

160.4	*G	160	0228	④Gordonsville____Va
165.3		VM89	0233	††Madison Run___Va
169.0		VM86	0235	So. Orange_____Va
169.4	*OH	VM85	0238	①④Orange_____Va
			0239	Orange Ticket
				Office_____Va
		VM79		Rapidan_____Va
		VM67		Culpeper_____Va
		VM46		Calverton_____Va
		VM33		Manassas_____Va
		VM23		Fairfax_____Va
	*Z	VM 7		Alexandria_____Va
	*YD		0245	①Potomac Yard__Va
254.1	*H	VM 0	0246	④Washington____D C
			0247	④Union Station_____
			0248	Baggage_____
			0249	④City Ticket Office,
	PA			714 14th St., N. W.
			0242	④Arlington_____Va

43

F-16s seemingly most common. After 1946 the class L-1 streamlined 4-6-4 Hudsons were also used, and, in fact, one of these streamlined engines operated the last steam-powered passenger trains on the line and ended steam operations there with a special excursion. Mountain type 4-8-2s were also used on trains east of Charlottesville into Washington as needed.

Freight in the early era was powered, of course, by 4-6-0s and 2-8-0s, with 2-8-2s coming after about 1912. In the later decades of steam the 2-10-2 Santa Fe types were most commonly used on freights between Charlottesville and Alexandria.

After coming of diesels, GP7s an GP9s were the usual power, with occasional F7s on through freights, supplanted in the late 1960s with second generation diesels. After January 1952 all passenger trains used E8s, generally in back-to-back sets of two, which continued until Amtrak's take-over in 1971.

Washington Union Terminal was the destination of C&O passenger trains after its construction in 1906. It fell on bad days with the decline of passenger trains, but has been revived, as a high volume commuter and Amtrak terminal and now is the most visited building in Washington. (C&O Ry. Photo, C&O Hist. Society Collection)

Profile of the Washington Subdivision shows a succession of heavy but very short grades in a hilly environment. (C&O Historical Society Collection)

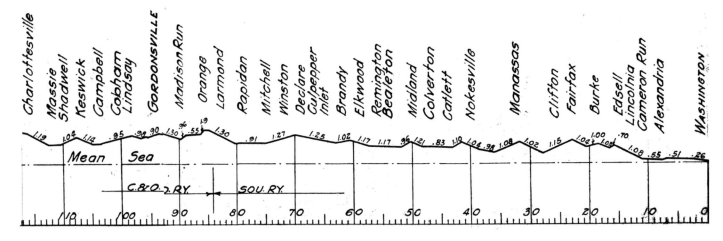

A Washington Union Terminal agent checks passengers through to board No. 1, the westbound George Washington in February 1947. The 6:01 departure time was never altered. (C&O Ry. Photo, C&O Hist. Society Collection)

Under PRR's wires, No. 5, the westbound Sportsman passes the Department of Agriculture building after emerging from the tunnel leading from the lower level trackage at Washington Union Terminal in 1955, led by E8 4021. (C&O Historical Society Collection, COHS-1125)

A great Sunday afternoon pastime in the 1950s was for people to sit on the lawn at Alexandria Union Station and watch the parade of C&O and Southern trains. Here No. 5/47 is leaving for the long run to Cincinnati in 1955. (C&O Historical Society Collection)

No. 1, The George Washington, *is leaving Alexandria in 1963 with the usual two E8s and eight cars. (Jim Shaw photo)*

J-2 class Mountain type No. 549 takes No. 5, The Sportsman, out of Orange in October 1937. Typical of the era, the big 4-8-2 is adorned with polished air pumps and cylinder heads and the cameo portrait of Washington. (J. I. Kelly Photo, C&O Hist. Society Collection, COHS-4100)

Z Tower in Alexandria is the seen here in the 1930s as the operator taps out a telegraphic message and a C&O train powered by a flying pumps Pacific thunders by outside. (TLC Collection)

A C&O train is headed into Washington under PRR wires with a heavily head-end consist including express cars, a full RPO, a working mail and baggage car and three passenger cars in this June 16, 1947 photo. F-18 No. 482 is power (Bruce Fales, Jay Williams collection)

Freight trains on the Washington Division is typified by this ca. 1949 photo with B-1 2-10-2 No. 2952 and a heavy merchandise train including a stock car and refrigerator car up front. (John Krause Photo, TLC Collection)

In another scene with a B-1 No. 2954 has an empty coal train at milepost VM 8.5 just south of Alexandria Sept. 24, 1950. (J. I. Kelly Photo, D. Wallace Johnson Collection)

5: Charlottesville

Charlottesville is associated with Virginia's old days through its connection with Thomas Jefferson, whose home, Monticello, overlooked the town. It was he who built the University of Virginia here, and his spirit has always infused the town, whose main business right up to the present has been learning–the university. This, of course, made it an important passenger traffic location for C&O.

Charlottesville was also associated with the agricultural region around it and that type of freight business was always plentiful. It was as well the location at which C&O connected with and crossed the Southern Railway's Washington–Atlanta–New Orleans mainline, so there was also interchange business.

However, the major importance of Charlottesville on the C&O was as a consist shifting and motive power change point for its passenger trains, after 1889 when the pattern of C&O passenger train operation was firmly established in the system that would endure to the end.

As the Louisa Railroad was contemplating a westward expansion beyond Gordonsville, two different towns wanted to be its next terminus: Harrisonburg and Charlottesville. After several years of indecision, the Charlottesville route was chosen, and tracks reached the town in the Spring of 1850, at about the same time that Louisa changed its name to Virginia Central. Tracks were immediately pressed westward, and breached the Blue Ridge with the state's help, reaching Jackson's River Station at the foot of the Alleghanies in 1857.

C&O was then completed through to the Ohio River in 1873 and on to Cincinnati in the late 1880s.

It was in 1889-90 that C&O was completely revitalized and a major program of expansion initiated. Improvement of the physical plant was undertaken by new management headed by President Melville E. Ingalls and his Morgan and Vanderbilt financial backers. C&O built new shops, yards, stations, bridges, yards, and track all across its system. As part of this, the James River line was acquired from the Richmond & Alleghany Railway in 1890, and all coal traffic headed to Newport News was diverted to that line away from the mountain line via Charlottesville. In 1889 a trackage rights agreement was effected between C&O and the Virginia Midland Railway (later Southern, now NS) so that C&O passenger and freight trains could use that line between Orange and Washington. Agreements were also made with the Pennsylvania Railroad to carry C&O's new luxury train, *The Fast Flying Virginian*, through to New York. These arrangements established a new focus for C&O passenger business.

No longer was the passenger traffic advertised and concentrated on the Cincinnati-Richmond-Newport News route, but now it was to be Cincinnati-Washington, with secondary, connecting service to Richmond and Newport News-Norfolk.

The logical break-point for the connection was at Charlottesville, the division point and yard about 20 miles west of where the Washington line joined the Richmond line (Washington SD and Piedmont SD).

Track chart showing layout of Charlottesville, including yard, stations, and engine terminal. Note Southern Railway crossing and Union Station at left. (C&O Historical Society Collection)

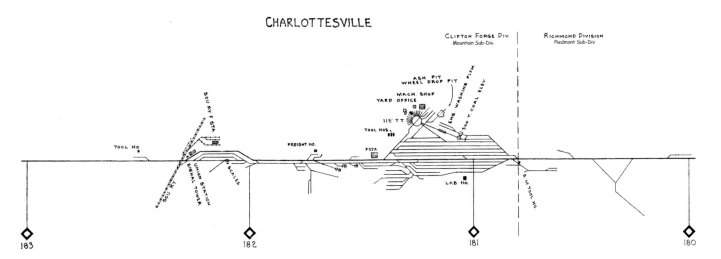

The magnificent 1905 C&O station on Main Street served all C&O trains and still stands today, now adaptively used by private business. (TLC Collection)

From that time onward the general pattern of C&O passenger traffic (see further data in chapter 12), was that trains originating in Cincinnati were joined with trains originating in Louisville at Ashland, Kentucky, sent east as a consolidated consist, then broken again at Charlottesville with the main section headed to Washington, and the Virginia section headed to Richmond and Newport News. Westbound the opposite occurred. This became the biggest part of Charlottesville's terminal operations for the next 80 years.

The pattern in the immediate post-WWII era was established so that this operation occurred with three sets of trains each day. Locals were also operated with Charlottesville either an end or intermediate terminal.

Freight consisted of the usual local freight trains serving the Piedmont, Mountain and Washington Subdivisions out of Charlottesville. Through freight trains headed to Potomac Yard in Alexandria were serviced and if necessary were worked at Charlottesville as well. The yard accommodated the freight business of the city and its environs, the shifting of through freights as needed, assembly of local freights, collection of interchange traffic with the Southern, etc. A coach yard was set up with necessary facilities for servicing passenger cars laying over between runs, and a branch of the C&O's commissary was established to take care of supplying dining cars on the route (the main commissary was at Ashland, Ky.).

A succession of smaller wooden frame depots served the city until 1905 when a large red brick station in neo-Classical or Georgian style was erected on Main Street. It was in front of this station with its long covered platform that the consist adjustment switching was done as each train paused.

Just to the east of the station a roundhouse with small attached machine shop and engine terminal/ready track area was available, as well as 300-ton concrete coaling station, which replaced an older wooden trestle style in the early 1920s.

Just under a mile west of the C&O station was the Southern Railway crossing and location of its station. In 1890 C&O and Southern jointly built a large new station here which thereafter was known as "Charlottesville Union Station," and after that time C&O trains made two stops, one at Union Station and one at the C&O station. The Union Station stop was to accommodate passengers transferring to and from Southern trains, and for university students, because this station was closest to the campus.

As the passenger business declined, and freight business in this region dried up in the 1960s, C&O operations were steadily downgraded, the roundhouse taken out of service, and after the end of C&O-operated passenger trains, the only remaining traffic was the one Amtrak train, some local car-load freight business, and a set of through freights to Potomac Yard and one over the Piedmont. Eventually, after CSX mergers, the trackage rights over the SR lapsed, and little was left. The yard was taken up and most everything is gone now except a few tracks now used by lessor Buckingham Branch Railroad, which operates the line. The fine old C&O station is now used as law offices, and only the large concrete coaling station stands as a reminder of the engine terminal. Union Station is now used by Amtrak trains on the old C&O line (now CSX) and on the Southern (now NS).

1926 photo of the small 6-stall Charlottesville roundhouse. (TLC Collection)

Inside the Charlottesville roundhouse in June 1946, B-1 class 2-10-2 No. 2958 is receiving some maintenance. The 2-10-2s were very common power at this terminal, being used on the Washington, Piedmont, and Mountain Subdivisions. (C&O Ry. Photo, C&O Hist. Society Collection, CSPR-606)

No. 4, The Sportsman, is becoming No. 4 and No. 46 as it is broken apart and reassembled at Charlottesville. The pair of E8s at right will handle the Washington section, while the single unit on the left will take the Virginia section to Richmond and Newport News, on April 23,1961. (Arthur B. Johnson, Photo, C&O Hist. Society Collection, COHS-29336)

Night scene looking west at the ready tracks in about 1959 shows E8s between runs, the roundhouse in background right, and GP9s left. Yard tracks are filled with freight to the left. One could always find E8s here as they were serviced and shifted among the trains being adjusted at this point. (TLC Collection)

J-3 No. 601 and K-4 No. 2764 are getting ready to handle passenger and freight trains respectively in a great 1949 scene at the Charlottesville ready tracks. (H. Reid Photo)

E8 4008 and mate have just arrived Charlottesville with **The Sportsman,** *No. 4/46 with a substantial consist of three head-end cars and eight passenger cars at 11:20 a.m. Feb. 14, 1953. The locomotive still has its coupler cowl in place. These were taken off when multiple-unit connections were added in 1959 so units could be operated three at a time. (R. R. Malinoski Photo)*

An elegant and sparkling J-3, No. 600, is poised to leave Charlottesville westbound in the late 1930s. The Greenbriers were principal power west of Charlottesville after they arrived in 1935. This particular engine was named "Th. Jefferson," and thus very appropriate to the locale. (Bruce D. Fales Photo)

Charlottesville Union Station in 1949. The SR mainline is just out of the photo at left, while the C&O is seen on the right. A joint station for passenger business, it was C&O's second stop in Charlottesville. (C&O Historical Society Collection, COHS-6541)

C&O J-3 4-84- N.602 is leaving Union Station westbound, passing JC Cabin and crossing the Southern diamonds with No. 5, the westbound Sportsman *in 1948. (H H. Harwood, Jr. Collection)*

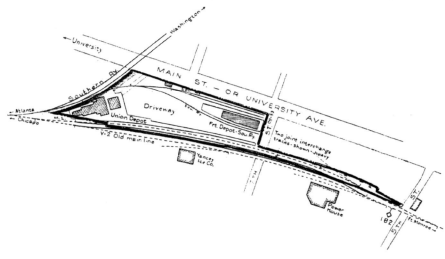

Track layout at Union Station. (C&O Hist. Society Collection)

6: The Rivanna Subdivision

The line of C&O rails between Richmond and Clifton Forge following the James River and passing through Lynchburg consists of two subdivisions, the Rivanna and the James River. They will be treated in this and the next two chapters.

What has always been called the James River Line consisted of the Rivanna Subdivision, running from Rivanna Junction, near Main Street Station in the city of Richmond, to the town of Gladstone, about half-way to the terminal at Clifton Forge. From Gladstone to Clifton Forge the line is called the James River Subdivision. The town of Gladstone was established strictly for the C&O to serve as the division point terminal between the two.

During the era following the War Between the States numerous railroads were projected, as canals were already in eclipse. Thus it was with the old James River & Kanawha Canal, which had been built from Richmond along the James River as far as Buchanan before the war. It had also operated a turnpike from that point on to the Ohio River (later US Route 60). The original plan, conceived by early Virginia businessmen and supported by George Washington, was to have a waterway following the James, crossing Alleghany Mountain, and following the westward-flowing rivers to the Ohio-Mississippi system. It was quite successful in the antebellum era, but by the 1850s it as recognized that a railroad would be needed instead of the canal to make the "Great Connection" between Tidewater and the "Western Waters." By this time the Virginia Central, C&O's predecessor had already reached the base of the Alleghanies and the advance of the canal was halted. However, even after the war the canal company attempted to revive itself. It was in 1881 that the canal finally gave up and the Richmond & Alleghany Railroad was built along its tow-path, thus symbolizing in a very concrete way how that the new railroad technology had taken the center stage.

The Richmond & Alleghany and the Buchanan & Clifton Forge Railroads were chartered in 1878 and 1876 respectively, to build the line between Richmond and Clifton Forge, following the river and the canal. The Buchanan & Clifton Forge was then merged into the R&A and the R&A built the line in 1881, but soon went into bankruptcy and receivership. Although the R&A had a much better route between Richmond and the west than did C&O, since its line had an easy grade following the James River, it had few sources for local traffic, be-

cause it ran though a largely agricultural region that possessed no large deposits of mineral resources. The R&A had hoped for a good through or overhead traffic, but C&O froze it out by refusing to give it good rates at Williamson's (present day Clifton Forge).

After struggling for almost a decade, the new Ingallls management of the C&O was able to acquire and merge the R&A in 1890. This gave the C&O a great new route that would prove to be one of its finest assets. Instead of having to haul very heavy coal trains over two steep mountain grades from Clifton Forge to Charlottesville, C&O could now send its coal on a gently descending river-level route to Richmond. This was much less expensive and troublesome, and immediately after the line was merged, it was upgraded and made ready for a heavy traffic. This traffic had been building as C&O's coalfields in southern West Virginia began to develop rapidly.

From the early 1890s onward, C&O sent its heavy coal trains east on the James River line, as well as fast freight with lading for Richmond and Newport News. This has remained so until today, and it serves as a main CSX coal route. The route never had any appreciable passenger business because of its rural nature and its single city of any population, Lynchburg. In the era of principal interest for this book, the mid-20th Century, there were only a couple of local passenger trains on the James River Line, handled by Brill Gas-Electric cars, while the heavy name trains continued to use the Mountain Subdivision to Charlottesville where they divided with a section headed to Washington and one to Richmond. The last gas-electric motor trains were discontinued in October 1957.

As part of the upgrade of the R&A's facilities after the 1890 merger, C&O built a terminal at Gladstone, about halfway between Clifton Forge and Richmond. The yard here served one main purpose, to stage coal trains headed for Newport News terminal, and to provide a small engine maintenance facility and crew change point.

The Rivanna Subdivision

East of Gladstone, the Rivanna Subdivision operated the main line and three connecting branch lines. At Bremo, about 66 miles west of Richmond, the Buckingham Branch connected. This had been built as the Buckingham Railroad and was merged into the R&A, thus came to the C&O with that line. It ran 16 miles to the agricultural town of Dillwyn.

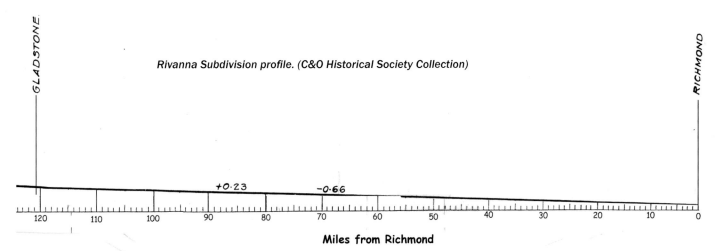

+0.23   −0.66

Miles from Richmond

It was incorporated in 1879, built between New Canton (opposite the C&O at Bremo) to Arvonia 1884-85, then from Arvonia to Rosney 1892-93. The trackage was eventually cut back to Dillwyn. Its business consisted of forest and farm products, and a type of slate which was widely used and constituted a considerable traffic. To reach the mainline there was a long bridge across the James River, since the branch ran almost due south from the river. This branch continued to be viable and valuable to C&O, and a new modern bridge was installed here after a hurricane-induced flood took the old one away. In 1989 it was sold to a private operator which runs the line very successfully today (2011) as the Buckingham Branch Railroad. This is the same operator who runs the former C&O Piedmont and Mountain Subdivisions.

Although the Buckingham Branch intersected the Rivanna Subdivision main line at Bremo, the terminal was at Strathmore, about half a mile to the west of the connection at Bremo. Here a station and engine servicing facilities were installed, and in the post-1920 period a huge concrete coaling station with a capacity of 500-tons was available for use by mainline and branch line trains. A small yard was built here, as well as bunk-house facilities and a water station. The reason that Strathmore was important was that in addition to its terminal operation for the Buckingham Branch, it was also the terminal for another branch line that ran almost directly north. This was called the Virginia Air Line Subdivision. It was built in 1906-08 as an independent railroad called the Virginia Air Line Railroad. Its name signified why it was built. In those days people spoke on the most direct line between two points as an "air line," much as we would say "as the crow flies." Many railroads used this in their names long before airplane transport was imagined. It was merged into C&O in 1912.

The Virginia Air Line Branch (VAL) ran from Strathmore 25 miles northward to Lindsay, a sta-

tion on C&O's Piedmont Subdivision about 15 miles east of Charlottesville. After the VAL was acquired by C&O and because it had no real local traffic to speak of, the C&O used it for a few specialty purposes. Whenever there was a large load that could not be sent over the Mountain Subdivision because of clearance problems in its tunnels, the load was sent down the VAL and over the James River line. Some freight headed to Potomac Yard at Alexandria, were routed down the James River line then up the VAL so as to avoid the Mountain Subdivision grades, including occasional coal trains. The VAL was finally abandoned in the 1960s as the mergers of the C&O/B&O era took effect making it no longer needed for its usual work.

The third branch connecting with the Rivanna Subdivision was the six-mile Alberene Subdivision between Warren on the main line and Alberene. It was also originally an independent railroad, built in 1897-98 and merged into C&O in 1902. Between Esmont and Alberene this branch was leased to the short line Nelson & Albemarle Railroad, which served the soapstone quarries of the region. The Nelson & Albemarle was built in 1902-04 to join the short line Schuyler Railway (serving another soapstone mine) and absorbed it in 1905. The N&A then leased and operated C&O's Alberene Branch between Esmont and Alberene and delivered its traffic to C&O at Esmont. N&A operated some interesting little saddle-tank steam locomotives, which were sometimes seen on the Alberene branch during interchange. In 1936 the line between Guthrie and Alberene was abandoned after the soapstone quarry closed. In 1948 the line between Schuyler and the Southern Railway connection was abandoned after a bridge wash-out. The soapstone plant at Schuyler was phased our and the line completely abandoned in 1963. The C&O then abandoned its Alberene SD trackage Warren to Esmont.

RIVANNA SUB-DIVISION

Dist. from Ft. Monroe	Tel. Calls	Sta-tion No.	Code No.	STATIONS
84.4		84		†Rivanna Jct._____Va
84.7		85	0125	①Richmond_____Va
	*JN			J. N. Cabin_____Va
	*DO			Dispatcher's Office__
			0128	④Main St. Station___
			0130	Baggage_____
88.9		A4	0307	‡Korah_____Va
91.9	*VA	A7	0309	Westham_____Va
93.9		A10	0312	†Bosher_____Va
95.6		A11	0315	†Mooreland_____Va
96.6		A12	0317	Lorraine_____Va
				‡Saunders Crossing Va
98.2		A13	0319	†Tuckahoe_____Va
100.1		A15	0320	Vinita_____Va
101.5		A17	0322	†Manakin_____Va
102.8		A18	0324	‡Harris Siding____Va
103.3		A19	0326	†Boscobel_____Va
105.9	*D	A20	0328	Sabot_____Va
106.4		A21	0329	Boice Siding____Va
109.2		A24	0332	Lee_____Va
111.6		A27	0334	State Farm_____Va
112.9		A28	0336	†Thorncliff_____Va
113.3		A29	0338	‡Mt. Bernard____Va
115.3	J	A30	0340	Maidens_____Va
117.4		A33	0342	†Cedar Point____Va
118.3		A34	0344	Irwin_____Va
122.6		A37	0348	†Ben Lomond____Va
124.9	*RC	A40	0351	Rock Castle_____Va
127.0		A42	0353	West View_____Va
129.1		A44	0355	†Stokes_____Va
131.3		A45	0357	†Selden_____Va
131.9	A	A47	0360	Pemberton_____Va
136.4	*KI	A52	0362	Elk Hill_____Va
138.6		A54	0364	Island_____Va
141.3	C	A57	0366	Columbia_____Va
144.0		A60	0370	†Rivanna_____Va
147.2		A62	0372	Stearnes_____Va
151.2	B	A66	0375	②Bremo_____Va
152.8	*SM	A68	0409	⑤Strathmore____Va
155.0		A70	0412	Shores_____Va
157.4		A73	0416	Hardware_____Va
159.8		A75	0418	†Paynes_____Va
161.8		A77	0420	††Nicholas_____Va
164.1	S	A79	0422	Scottsville_____Va
167.5		A83	0424	Hatton_____Va
170.2	RN	A85	0428	②Warren_____Va
175.8	HN	A91	0441	Howardsville____Va
178.6		A94	0443	Highland_____Va
180.8		A96	0445	Manteo_____Va
183.9	*WR	A99	0448	Warminster____Va
186.7		A102	0451	Midway_____Va
188.7	H	A104	0453	Wingina_____Va
193.4	W	A109	0455	Norwood_____Va
195.6		A111	0457	Buffalo Station__Va
198.8		A114	0461	Greenway_____Va
202.8		A118	0463	Caskie_____Va
203.8	*GS	A119	0465	Gladstone_____Va

†—No Siding.
††—Passing Siding only.
‡—Private Siding only.
④—Coupon Stations.
*—Day and Night Telegraph Offices.
①—Junction with connecting lines.
②—Junctions of Sub-division shown elsewhere.

Statistics

Mainline trackage - 119.1 miles
Stations: 52 named locations (1948)

Branches:
Buckingham Subdivision: 16.4 miles

Alberene Subdivision: 6.1 miles
Virginia Air Line Subdivision: 29.2 miles

Opposite Left: Rivanna Subdivision Station List (1948).

Opposite Right: In this scene we see the C&O's Rivanna Subdivision trackage just east of Richmond, with a train switching the Albemarle Paper Company, in September 1946. The old JR&K Canal is between the two sets of tracks at this point. C&O kept water in the canal at this location as part of an agreement to supply it to the city and to some other industries in the area. (C&O Ry. Photo, C&O Historical Society Collection, CSPR-683)

Opposite Below: First No. 92, a regularly scheduled coal train (!), had Mikado No. 1232 passing milepost 6 on the Rivanna Subdivision headed into Richmond on May 9, 1947, near Westham station. (J. I. Kelly Photo, D. Wallace Johnson Collection)

Right: K-3 Mikado No. 1257 has a westbound manifest train leaving Richmond in September 1947 with the skyline in the hazy distance. (C&O Ry. Photo, C&O Historical Society Collection, CSPR-1175)

This is an unusual scene. J-3A No. 613 was one of two C&O locomotives that had "elephant ear" smoke deflectors installed about 1950. After it was taken out of passenger service with the arrival of the E8 diesels it went to work for a short time on James River Line trains, seen here on the Rivanna Subdivision near Westham station October 19, 1952. (H. Reid Photo)

In most Rivanna and James River scenes the river is present. Just west of Richmond in April 1952, K-3a 2-8-2 No. 2329 takes a mainly empty coal train west with some box and gondola cars up front. (J. I. Kelly photo, C&O Historical Society Collection, COHS-313)

An eastbound manifest freight is double-heading with K-3 Mikados (1214 in the lead), blasting past the Bremo station November 3, 1950, with a heavy cut of refrigerator cars up front. (J. D. Welsh photo, C&O Historical Society Collection)

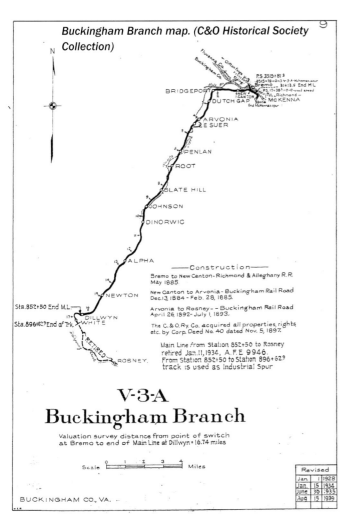

Buckingham Branch map. (C&O Historical Society Collection)

V-3-A
Buckingham Branch

Valuation survey distance from point of switch
at Bremo to end of Main Line at Dillwyn = 16.74 miles

—Construction—

Bremo to New Canton-Richmond & Alleghany R.R.
May 1885.

New Canton to Arvonia-Buckingham Rail Road
Dec.13, 1884 - Feb. 28, 1885.

Arvonia to Rosney - Buckingham Rail Road
April 26 1892-July 1, 1893.

The C. & O.Ry. Co. acquired all properties, rights
etc. by Corp. Deed No. 40 dated Nov. 5, 1897.

Main Line from Station 852+50 to Rosney
retired Jan.11, 1934, A.F.E. 9946.
From Station 852+50 to Station 896+62.9
track is used as Industrial Spur

Scale 0 1 2 3 4 Miles

BUCKINGHAM CO., VA.

Revised		
Jan.	1	1928
Jan.	15	1934
June	30	1935
Aug	15	1939

K-3 Mikado No. 1232 is powering a coal train near Bremo in May 1951. The powerful 2-8-2s in the K-2, K-3, and K-3a classes were used most commonly on trains over the James River line after they arrived in 1923-1925, right up to the end of steam in the early 1950s. (C&O Historical Society Collection)

On September 4, 1950, G-7 class 2-8-0 No. 884 has a Buckingham Branch train crossing the James River bridge at New Canton en route to Dillwyn from Strathmore and Bremo on the Rivanna Subdivision on the other side of the river. (D. Wallace Johnson Photo)

In this view the Buckingham Branch locomotive is in the middle of its train in order to facilitate shifting before crossing the bridge. Note hoppers and gondolas for the stone products and pulp wood bulkhead flats in the rear for this other big commodity handled on the line. Note that this is a mixed train, with its old wooden combination car. (J. I. Photo, D. Wallace Johnson Collection)

The station at Dillwyn, principal point and terminal on the Buckingham Branch, is seen here in November 1950, as the mixed train has been reassembled for its trip back to Bremo and Strathmore. Today (2011) the station is used as headquarters for the Buckingham Branch Railroad Company). (J. I. Kelly Photo, C&O Historical Society Collection, COHS-31)

DILLWYN

Bedford Pulp & Paper Co.

Industrial Lead

Burrus Land & Lbr. Co.

C.C. Camden

◇ 17

End of Main Line

Siding

House

DEPOT

Barnes Lumber Co.

Main Track

To Bremo

Seay Mill Co

Standard Oil Co.

Dunlap Tobacco Co.

⊥⊥

□ 16

Retired

Calls	Hours Open	Distance from Bremo	SECOND CLASS. 307 Mixed Daily Ex. Sun.	TIMETABLE No. 136. In Effect Sunday, April 30, 1950. STATIONS.	SECOND CLASS. 308 Mixed Daily Ex. Sun.	Side Track Capacity in Cars (41 ft.)
	WESTWARD			BUCKINGHAM SUBDIVISION	EASTWARD	
B	8.00a.m. to 5.00p.m. Ex. Sunday	.0	L AM 9 45	W **BREMO**	A PM 1 20	-----
------	------------	4.0	f10 10	4.0 Arvonia	f12 59	o18
------	------------	9.4	f10 30	5.4 Johnson	f12 37	o11
------	------------	16.4	11 00 308 t A AM	7.0 **DILLWYN**	12 10 307 L PM	o97
			307 Mixed Daily Ex. Sun.	No. 307 is Superior to No. 308, Bremo to Dillwyn.	**308** Mixed Daily Ex. Sun.	

Bremo station, water tank, signals, and ancillary structures make a neat rural scene in this November 1950 photo looking west. The high bridge in the background is US Route 15. The Buckingham Branch line comes in to the west and isn't quite visible. (J. D. Welsh Photo, C&O Historical Society Collection, COHS-1241)

BREMO

East End of 2nd Track

← West

W.B.M.L.

E.B.M.L.

To Dillwyn →

Buckingham S.D.

Loading

Depot

Loading

Main Track

Storage

End of Track

6 6

Track layout at Bremo. (C&O Historical Society Collection)

The Strathmore terminal was a small, compact facility that had everything. In this photo, looking west on March 21, 1953, the Buckingham Branch G-7 is being serviced. The small station is to the left background. Water column (tank in background) cinder conveyor, inspection pits, stand house, and other structures are all in place. The structure the roofs of which can be seen in the background are the bunkhouse for crews laying over here. (D. Wallace Johnson Photo)

Strathmore yard with is wye track for turning locomotives, at coaling station (right), as well as the VAL line at right. (C&O Historical Society Collection)

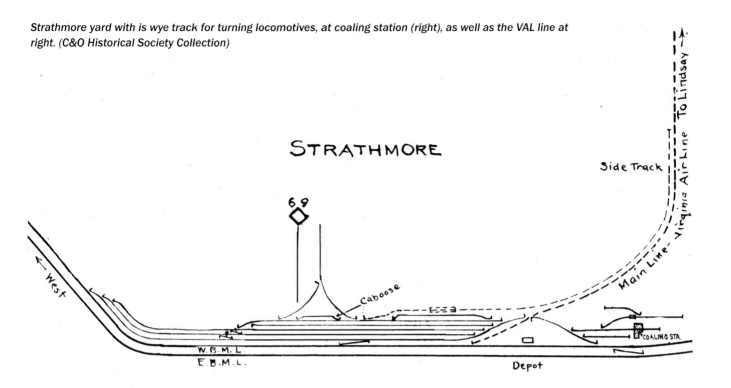

The large 500-ton concrete coaling station was for use by the branch line trains, but principally for the mainline trains, since the run of 119 miles between Richmond and Gladstone was one of the longer runs on the C&O. K-3a No. 2312 is heading east in this July 28, 1951 photo (C&O Historical Society Collection)

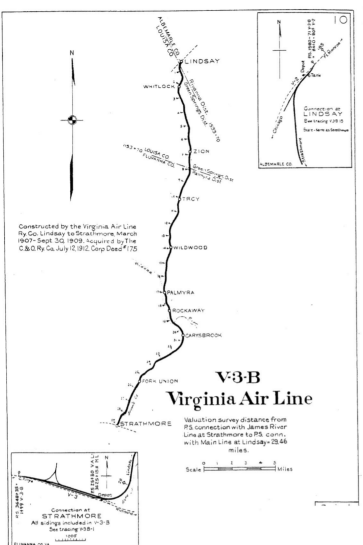

V·3·B
Virginia Air Line

Valuation survey distance from
P.S. connection with James River
Line at Strathmore to P.S. conn.
with Main Line at Lindsay = 29.46
miles.

Scale |0 1 2 3 4 5| Miles

Constructed by the Virginia Air Line
Ry. Co. Lindsay to Strathmore, March
1907 - Sept. 30, 1909. Acquired by The
C. & O. Ry. Co. July 12, 1912. Corp. Deed #175.

VIRGINIA AIR LINE SUB-DIVISION

165.2	*DA	165	0250	Lindsay_____	Va
168.7		V3	0255	Thelma_____	Va
171.9		V6	0258	Zion_____	Va
173.4	CN	V8	0260	Kays_____	Va
175.2		V10	0262	Troy_____	Va
178.9		V13	0265	Wildwood_____	Va
181.9		V16	0268	Palmyra_____	Va
183.7		V18	0271	Rockaway_____	Va
185.7		V20	0275	Carysbrook_____	Va
190.6		V25	0279	Fork Union_____	Va
194.4	*SM	A68	0409	Strathmore_____	Va

④–Coupon Stations.
*–Day and Night Telegraph Offices.
①–Junction with connecting lines.
②–Junction of Sub-division shown elsewhere.

VAL Branch station list (1948)

Map of VAL Subdivision showing its line between Strathmore on the Rivanna Subdivision and Lindsay on the Piedmont. (C&O Historical Society Collection)

Map of the
NELSON
and ALBEMARLE
Railway Company

AND CONNECTIONS

(not to scale)

A — (Rockfish to Schuyler) Originally
built as Schuyler Railway; abandoned in 1948.

B — (Guthrie to Esmont) Leased to N&A
by C&O; abandoned in 1963.

C — (Guthrie to Alberene) Leased to
N&A by C&O; abandoned in 1936.

D — (Esmont to Warren) Operated for
C&O by N&A; abandoned about 1963.

Information for map from Charles H. Cox.

This map, which was prepared by Carl Shaver for the C&O Historical Society Newsletter, shows the relationship of the Alberene Subdivision, the Nelson & Albemarle Railroad, and the C&O and Southern Railway mainlines. (C&O Historical Society Collection)

Alberene Subdivision station list, 1948.

ALBERENE SUB-DIVISION

170.2	RN	A85	0428	Warren_____Va
172.3		J2	0430	Boiling Spring___Va
174.2		J4	0432	Dawson Mill_____Va
176.3		J6	0435	①Esmont_____Va

RICHMOND DIVISION
VIRGINIA AIR LINE SUBDIVISION

WESTWARD   EASTWARD

Calls	Hours Open	Distance from Lindsay	THIRD CLASS.		TIMETABLE No. 136. In Effect Sunday, April 30, 1950. STATIONS.	THIRD CLASS.		Side Track Capacity in Cars (41 ft.)
			95 Daily	**403** Mixed Daily Ex. Sun.		**98** Daily	**404** Mixed Daily Ex. Sun.	
			L	PM L	PM	A AM A	AM	
____	_____	.0	5 35	1 25	y LINDSAY	4 00	f 8 30	o372
					10.2			
CN	8.00a.m. to 5.00p.m. Ex. Sat. and Sun.	10.2	5 56	f 1 45	Troy	3 42	f 8 10	p125o9
					W—— 10.4			
____	_____	20.6	6 17	f 2 05	Carysbrook	3 10	f 7 35	p85o16
					4.9			
____	_____	25.5	6 27	f 2 15	Fork Union	3 00	f 7 20	o 7
					3.8			
SM	Continuous	29.3	6 45	2 25	Wy STRATHMORE	2 45	7 00	Yard
			A PM	A PM		L AM	L AM	
			95 Daily	**403** Mixed Daily Ex. Sun.		**98** Daily	**404** Mixed Daily Ex. Sun.	

This employee timetable entry for VAL Subdivision April 30, 1950, shows the mixed train each way and through fast freights No. 95 and 98. (C&O Employee Timetable, Richmond, Division No. 136, April 30, 1950)

K-2 2-8-2 No. 1200 is seen here picking up orders from the operator at the neat little station at Palmyra. This is mixed train No. 404, which took care of passenger and freight business along the line, seen here on September 26, 1951. (J. I. Kelly Photo, C&O Historical Society Collection)

The C&O depot at Esmont, where C&O operations stopped and N&A operations started, as it looked in its last days in 1961. (T. King photo, C&O Historical Society Collection)

The Nelson & Albemarle had a number of small saddle-tank locomotives to handle the soapstone business from its quarries to the C&O at Esmont. Here 2-4-2 No. 11 is at the engine house at Schuyler May 28, 1950. (TLC Collection)

7: Gladstone

Headquarters for C&O operations at Gladstone was this two-story frame station and office building erected in 1889, when the yard was built. The low cinderblock building to the right was the "new" Railroad YMCA that replaced the original wooden structure. The engine terminal is in the background. This photo taken in 1972. Today the station still stands, boarded up, and the yard still has several tracks, but all else is gone. The YMCA is now a community center. (T. W. Dixon, Jr. photo, C&O Historical Society Collection, COHS-9519)

Gladstone yard diagram shows the various tracks that were principally used to stage coal loads headed to Newport News. (C&O Historical Society Collection)

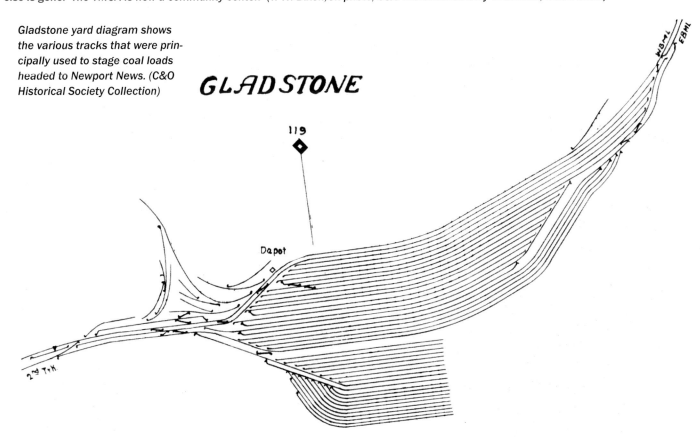

The small engine house at Gladstone as it appeared April 25, 1953, with the depot in the right distance, and the old YMCA behind it. An 0-8-0 sits at left on one leg of the wye track. (D. Wallace Johnson Photo)

A variety of first and second generation diesels populate the Gladstone ready tracks in 1973, with the wreck crane at left. (T. W. Dixon, Jr. Photo)

One of the most interesting facilities at Gladstone was the usual silo style 300-ton concrete coaling station and the tiny sand tower just beside. The hopper cars include two C&O Cinder Hoppers, numbered C24 and C26. These were old hoppers that were put to use strictly for carrying cinders away from engine terminals. The cinder conveyor is dumping into C24 at right. Cinders were often used as ballast on branch lines and as fill material. The abandoned coaling tower still stands. (D. Wallace Johnson Photo)

8: The James River Subdivision

Running between Gladstone and Clifton Forge, the James River Subdivision had about the same rural complexion as the Rivanna, as it ran along the bank of the James River. It had two branches. The first was the Lexington Subdivision, which ran from Balcony falls on the Rivanna to the town of Lexington, famous for its Washington & Lee University, and Virginia Military Institute. The town had been connected to the James River by the North River Navigation canal, and when the R&A was built it also built a branch along this canal to Lexington. This branch was built in 1881 by the Richmond & Alleghany.

When the Baltimore & Ohio tried its "southern strategy" by building a line down the Shenandoah Valley, it reached as far south as Staunton and Lexington, and connected with the C&O at both locations. C&O's actual station was called "East Lexington," and was about a mile from the main section of the town. In 1883 B&O built a large impressive brick depot in the town reminiscent of structures that it was building in northern West Virginia and Maryland in the 1880s. B&O's "Valley Line" carried a respectable traffic but was abandoned back to Staunton during WWII and then its line south of Harrisonburg was taken over by the Chesapeake Western during WWII. When B&O left Lexington, C&O assumed the trackage into the town, abandoned its East Lexington station and took over the former B&O depot, which it used to the end of its service to the town.

In 1905 C&O contracted with the Norfolk & Western Railway to handle its trains from Glasgow (called Balcony Falls on the C&O) to Buena Vista, a distance of 9 miles, at which point C&O trains then used the old Lexington Branch rails on into Lexington. This arrangement remained in effect until 1969 when the C&O portion of the line was washed out by a Hurricane Camille. It was abandoned and turned into a hiking trail at that time. The former C&O (originally B&O) station at Lexington is extant, having been moved away from the old right of way and is now reused for other purposes. The Lexington line in the mid-20th Century decades was served by a mixed train which carried a little freight and ancient wooden combination car for the few passengers. On occasion the students from the schools would need extra accommodation, and special trains or cars would be operated.

The other branch on the James River Subdivision was the Craig Valley Subdivision, intersecting the James River main line at Eagle Rock (earlier called Eagle Mountain). Iron was the reason for this branch. In the early 1890s, it was thought that Virginia would become the next great iron producing region for the country. Iron furnaces had been operating in the western Virginia mountains since the antebellum years, and it was thought that the large deposits of ore that underlay this region would be important for the industrializing country. C&O followed this logic when it built the Craig Valley line from Eagle Rock to Craig City (now New Castle), running about 25 miles along Craig Creek.

Mines were operated at Oriskany, 15 miles up the line, and at Barbour's Creek, about 21 miles along the branch. By 1923 this mine had produced 938,560 tons of ore, a good showing but hardly a large operation by objective standards. When the Low Moor Iron Company ceased its operations at Low Moor and

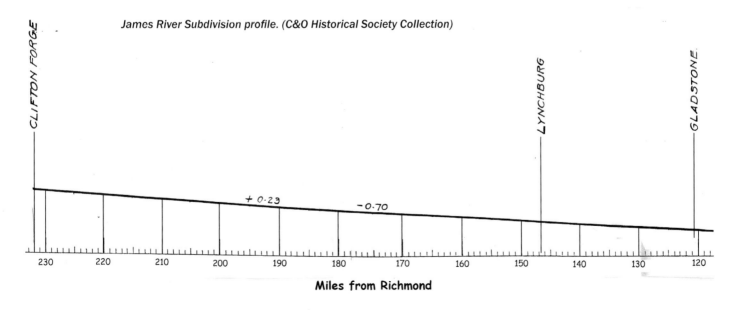

James River Subdivision profile. (C&O Historical Society Collection)

Miles from Richmond

Covington in 1926, all mining operations on the line stopped. From that time forward the Craig Valley Branch was largely a supplier of pulp wood for the big paper mill at Covington, and for the usual rural agricultural branch line traffic. In the era of this book C&O operated a three times weekly mixed train with a few cars of freight and an old wooden combination car for a passenger or two now and then until 1954 when the passenger car was discontinued. The line continued its operation with steadily declining revenue until 1961 when it was abandoned and taken up. The right-of-way was sold to the Commonwealth of Virginia which turned parts of it into a state highway. Some of the bridges on the line were preserved and though no longer used by the highway still stand as the oldest C&O bridge structures still in existence, dating from the 1880s. They were moved to the Craig Valley line when it was built because at that time the lighter bridges were being removed from the main line as they were replaced with heavy structures.

The Craig Valley's terminal was Clifton Forge. Trains originated at Clifton Forge, traveled the 20 miles over the James River Subdivision track to Eagle Rock, and then up the branch. Because of the light bridges C&O used small steam locomotives. In the early 1930s it brought in two 4-6-0 Ten Wheelers which had been acquired when the Chicago, Cincinnati & Louisville was merged to become the C&O's Chicago Division in 1910. Numbered 377 and 378, they carried the traffic of the line and the Lexington branch for many years. No. 377 survives at the Baltimore & Ohio Museum in Baltimore.

The James River Subdivision main line had the same traffic that the Rivanna line did, with only a break at Gladstone. At Clifton Forge the old R&A line had run along the south bank of the Jackson River for a little over a mile and crossed the River into what was the main C&O yard in the 1880s, but later became the Smith Creek Yard and LCL freight area in the 1890s. A new bridge was erected by C&O across the Jackson River and it thereafter entered the main Clifton Forge yard at JD Cabin, the same junction as the Mountain Subdivision.

Motive Power on both the James River and Rivanna Subdivisions in the early era was mainly 2-8-0s with some 4-4-0s and 4-6-0s on the local passenger trains. By the 1915-1920 era 2-8-2s began handling steadily heavier coal trains eastward and empties back west, then when new K-2, K-3, and K-3a classes of 2-8-2 Mikados arrived in 1923-25 they became the standard power on both subdivisions. They had enough power to get a very heavy coal train east because of the favorable eastbound grades. After the coming of the K-4 class 2-8-4 Kanawhas they were also used on this line. In the early 1950s some J-3 class 4-8-4s were used on the line after they had been bumped off the passenger trains by the arrival of E8 diesels in early 1952.

F-15 class 4-6-2s eventually handled the passenger locals, but in 1930 these were replaced by new Brill gas-electric motor cars and trailers, which handled the locals until the end in 1957.

With the coming of diesels the ubiquitous GP7 and GP9 units handled coal and manifest freights on the line until the arrival of second generation units in the late 1960s an early 1970s. Some F7s were occasionally used on manifest freights. Today (2011) CSX powers its trains with back-to-back sets of very high horsepower GE and EMD units.

The depot at Big Island was similar to many that C&O inherited from the Richmond & Alleghany. They featured a squared bay window and hipped roof. Most of these buildings lasted to the end. This photo was taken in 1932. The industry in the background was a paper mill, which is now a huge operation, owned by Georgia Pacific. It has supplied large amounts of freight to C&O and to CSX even today. (C&O Historical Society Collection)

JAMES RIVER SUB-DIVISION

Dist. from Ft. Monroe	Tel. Calls	Station No.	Code No.	STATIONS
203.8	*GS	A119	0465	Gladstone_____Va
205.1		A120	0579	Allen Creek_____Va
207.8		A123	0581	Riverville_____Va
211.0		A126	0583	Walkerford_____Va
215.6		A131	0585	Stapleton_____Va
218.1		A133	0587	Galt's Mill_____Va
221.1		A136	0589	††Joshua Falls____Va
224.2		A139	0591	†Deacon_____Va
225.0		A140	0593	†Six Mile_____Va
225.8		A141	0594	Kelly_____Va
228.3		A144	0596	Tyree_____Va
231.0		A146	0598	①Lynchburg (F.D.) Va
231.3	*ND		0593	④ " Union Station____
232.2		A147		" So. R'y Crossing. City Tkt. Office__
			0595	
235.1	RM	A150	0602	Reusens_____Va
235.5		A151	0604	‡Judith Dam_____Va
239.0		A154		††G. W. Cabin____Va
239.4	RK	A155	0606	Abert_____Va
243.0		A158	0608	Holcomb Rock___Va
244.1		A159	0610	Pearch_____Va
245.5		A161	0612	Coleman_____Va
245.8		A161½	0613	Logan_____Va
248.6		A164	0615	Waugh_____Va
250.2	BD	A165	0617	Big Island_____Va
251.7	M	A167	0619	Major_____Va
255.4		A171	0622	Snowden_____Va
260.2	*K	A175	0626	②Balcony Falls___Va
261.1		A176	0640	‡Locher_____Va
262.1		A177	0642	†Virginia Manor___Va
262.8	VM	A178	0643	④Natural Bridge_Va
265.9		A181	0647	Gilmore Mills____Va
269.8	AP	A185	0649	Alpine_____Va
270.8		A186	0651	‡Rocky Point_____Va
273.6		A189	0653	Indian Rock_____Va
276.5		A192	0655	††Dillon_____Va
280.1	*BN	A195	0657	④Buchanan_____Va
284.2		A199	0662	Springwood_____Va
283.5		A198½		†J. N. Cabin_____Va
287.9		A203	0664	Lyle_____Va
290.0		A205	0666	†Saltpetre_____Va
291.9		A207	0669	†All_____Va
293.0		A208	0671	†Salisbury_____Va
294.8		A210	0673	††Dunn_____Va
297.2	*RA	A212	0675	②Eagle Rock_____Va
301.4		A217	0712	Gala_____Va
304.0		A219	0714	Haden_____Va
305.7		A221	0716	†Baldwin_____Va
308.2		A223	0718	Glen Wilton_____Va
310.9		A226	0720	†Lick Run_____Va
313.0		A228	0722	Iron Gate_____Va
314.2	*JD	A229		J. D. Cabin_____Va
277.5	*F	277	0577	④Clifton Forge____Va

①–Junction with connecting lines.
②–Junction of Sub-division shown elsewhere.
④–Coupon Stations.
*–Day and Night Telegraph Offices.
†–No Siding.
††–Passing Siding only.
‡–Private Siding only.

The James River and Rivanna Subdivisions remain a critically important CSX line today, carrying mainly eastbound coal traffic. Most westbound empty trains are sent over the Piedmont and Mountain Subdivisions, now operated by the Buckingham Branch Railroad.

Statistics

Mainline trackage - 110.4 miles
Stations: 47 named locations (1948)

Branches:
Lexington Subdivision: 20.8 miles
Crag Valley Subdivision: 36.9 miles

Connections: N&W at Balcony Falls, Loch Laird, Buena Vista, and Lynchburg; Southern at Lynchburg.

James River Subdivision Station list (1948)

In a great scene from 1881 near Lynchburg the bateaus on the JR&K Canal are making their last trips. The crossties for the new R&A at stacked along the tow-path which will form the R&A's roadbed. (C&O Historical Society Collection, CSPR-4635)

The largest city on the whole James River Line was Lynchburg, about 27 miles west of Gladstone. This panoramic photo shows the river front area of the city with its industries, warehouses, and railroads: (1) Huge C&O freight station and LCL yard; (2) Norfolk & Western freight station and LCL yard; (3) Union Station serving N&W, C&O, and some Southern Railway trains. Southern's main station in Lynchburg was at Kemper Street, some distance from this scene. C&O's Sandy Hook yard, a fairly small facility, is out of the photo to the left (4), while N&W's main yard was on Perceval's Island out in the river to the left out of the scene. (TLC Collection)

This late era photo shows the layout of facilities at Balcony Falls. These included a 100,000 gallon standpipe water tank and 300 Ton concrete coaling station as well as the depot, set between the main line tracks. (TLC Collection)

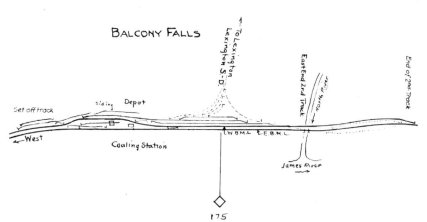

BALCONY FALLS

Balcony Falls track chart showing various tracks and Lexington Subdivision connection. (C&O Historical Society Collection)

K-3 No. 1257 brings an empty coal train west at Balcony Falls on May 10, 1951, while box cars for N&W interchange sit on adjacent track. (John Krause Photo)

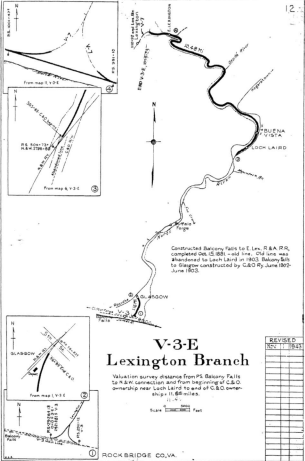

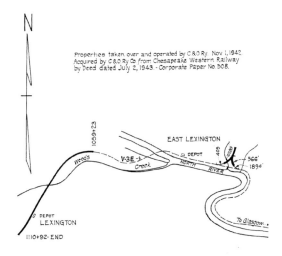

Lexington Branch map showing joint trackage with N&W from Glasgow to Loch Laird and C&O trackage into East Lexington. (C&O Historical Society Collection)

Map showing how C&O acquired trackage from Chesapeake Western (formerly B&O) into Lexington in 1942. At that time the C&O abandoned its East Lexington Station. The ex-B&O trackage beyond the end shown was abandoned back to Harrisonburg. (C&O Historical Society Collection)

Opposite Top and Above: In later years a GP7 replaced the 2-8-0 on the Lexington branch mixed train seen here in May 1953 headed away from Lexington with quite a bit of freight. (J. R. Kean Photos)

LEXINGTON SUB-DIVISION

260.2	*K	A175	0626	Balcony Falls	Va
261.3		B0	0627	Montridge	Va
			0628	①Glasgow	Va
			0629	Emil	Va
			0630	†Agnor	Va
			0631	Buffalo Forge	Va
			0641	†Thompson	Va
270.4		B10	0632	Loch Laird	Va
271.3	QN	B11	0633	①①**Buena Vista**	Va
275.1		B16	0635	South River	Va
278.7	AX	B20	0637	East Lexington	Va
281.0	XN	B21	0638	①**Lexington**	Va

Note.—Glasgow, Emil Siding, Agnor, Buffalo Forge, Terrace and Thompson are on joint track (N. & W.) between Balcony Falls and Loch Laird. Glasgow is the connection for loaded or empty cars for points north of Buena Vista and south of Glasgow, except for points on Branch west of Buena Vista.

N. & W. Joint Tracks, 261.6 to 269.8.
†–No Siding.
①–Coupon Stations.
*–Day and Night Telegraph Offices.
①–Junction with connecting lines.

Lexington Subdivision Station List (1948)

C&O's mixed train to Lexington is shown leaving that town for Balcony Falls in the winter of 1949 with its old wooden combine car. (J. Randolph Kean Photo)

The huge ex-B&O depot (built 1883) at Lexington as it looked in 1950. The building has been saved and moved to a different nearby location for adaptive reuse. (Ed Weber Photo)

Rolling up the line near Natural Bridge station in October 1954 is C&O Gas Electric motor train No. 9043 with trailing combine car. The James River locals were handled by Brill gas-electric motor cars (later converted to diesel) from 1930 until discontinuance in the fall of 1957. (J. R. Kean Photo, C&O Historical Society Collection, COHS-3376)

The stylish New Castle (originally Craig City) depot at the end of the Craig Valley Branch is seen here in 1961 boarded up. The branch trackage is in process of being taken up. (C&O Ry. Photo, C&O Historical Society)

CRAIG VALLEY SUB-DIVISION

297.2	*RA	A212	0675	Eagle Rock_____	Va
298.5		D1	0676	†Whitten_____	Va
301.3		D4	0680	Stull_____	Va
304.5		D6	0682	†Horton_____	Va
304.8		D7	0684	Parr_____	Va
305.9		D8	0686	†Hipes_____	Va
308.3		D10	0688	Lemon_____	Va
309.4		D12	0690	†Surber_____	Va
311.8		D13	0692	†Ruble_____	Va
312.8		D15	0695	Oriskany_____	Va
316.0		D18	0698	†Charlton_____	Va
317.3		D20	0700	†Given_____	Va
319.1		D21	0702	Barbour's Creek_	Va
320.7		D23	0704	†Marshalltown____	Va
321.3		D24	0706	†Virginia Mineral Springs_____	Va
322.3		D25	0708	†Pine Top_____	Va
324.1	CY	D26	0710	New Castle_____	Va

Craig Valley Branch station list (1948)

S-2 Alco diesel switcher No. 5067 handles the Craig Valley Branch local train in June 1952 which was a Tuesday-Wednesday-Thursday mixed train. By this time about the only commodity hauled was a bit of pulpwood. The line was abounded in 1961 to become a Virginia state highway. (Gene Huddleston Photo, C&O Historical Society Collection, COHS-2439)

Wasp Rock Tunnel is one of two on the James River Subdivision, seen here as eastbound manifest freight No. 90 passes through in 1978. (Aubrey Wiley Photo)

K-3a Mikado No. 2335 brings a coal train east past the typical C&O cantilever signal tower at the east end of the passing siding at Eagle Rock in June 1952. (Gene Huddleston Photo, C&O Historical Society Collection, COHS-1044)

J-3a 4-8-4 Greenbrier type No. 614 leads a coal train along the James River Subdivision in the summer of 1952 after having been bumped off passenger trains by the new E8s earlier that year. (Gene Huddleston Photo, C&O Historical Society Collection)

An empty coal train with a K-3a Mikado is crossing the Jackson River bridge at JD Cabin as it enters Clifton Forge yard in March 1949. The famous "Rainbow Rock" is in the background. The Mountain Subdivision mainline tracks are headed toward Charlottesville at left. (C&O Ry. Photo, C&O Historical Society Collection, CSPR-2334)

9: The Mountain Subdivision

This chapter covers the Mountain Subdivision line between Charlottesville at Clifton Forge. It was originally built by the Virginia Central in the 1850s, and today (2011) is leased to the Buckingham Branch Railroad for operation.

C&O's Mountain Subdivision ran between Charlottesville and Clifton Forge, and in so doing crossed two important mountain barriers, Blue Ridge Mountain and North Mountain. It left the Piedmont plain at Charlottesville, climbed over the Blue Ridge, then crossed the wide and verdant Shenandoah Valley, ascended Little North Mountain through a gap with favorable grades (but that were nonetheless the steepest on the C&O main line), then dipped and crossed other ridges before finally descending into Clifton Forge, its western terminal.

The Mountain Subdivision was part of the original Virginia Central main line, built in the mid-1850s. As explained in Chapter 3, the Louisa Railroad changed its name to Virginia Central as it completed its line of road into Charlottesville. In the late 1840s there had been considerable discussion as to which way the railroad would build once it left Gordonsville. One strong group wanted it to build to Harrisonburg, but another group favoring Charlottesville won out.

The first important consideration for the Virginia Central was how it would cross the formidable Blue Ridge barrier that stood immediately in its path west of Charlottesville. The fledgling company had limited

resources and it was not likely that enough money could be raised from the local rural countryside to carry forward the heavy work. At this point the Commonwealth of Virginia stepped in again as part of its policy of encouraging "internal improvements." The government wanted to help projects that would help "economic development," within Virginia. Therefore, the Blue Ridge Railroad was incorporated as a wholly state-owned company, with the sole task of building a line across the Blue Ridge from Mechem's River to a point near Waynesboro. It was to connect with the Virginia Central at Mechem's River in the east and Waynesboro in the west. This left the Virginia Central free to use its resources to continue building its line west of Waynesboro. By the time the Blue Ridge Railroad was completed, it was to be connected to an already existing line running to the west. The Virginia Central was to pay a toll to the Commonwealth for exclusive use of the Blue Ridge Railroad until its cost had been repaid. The Blue Ridge Railroad was finally sold to the new C&O in the 1870s.

As the Blue Ridge Railroad was being built, Virginia Central pushed its tracks west from Waynesboro, reaching Staunton in 1854, Millboro in 1856, and Jackson's River Station (near Clifton Forge) in 1857. While this work was being done, the Blue Ridge Railroad was being built with considerable difficulty because of the steep grades that were encountered and the necessity to bore several tunnels. The principal work of the line, however, was the boring of Blue Ridge Tunnel, at the top of the grade near the town of Afton.

This condensed profile shows the problems encountered by trains operating in both directions over the Mountain Subdivision. The stiffest eastbound from Clifton Forge was to reach North Mountain at 1.43%, then to reach Blue Ridge Tunnel another 1.43%, and in between several of almost this severity. Westbound the worst grade was 1.60% from Swoope to North Mountain. It's easy to see why the James River line was so much better for eastbound coal (see Chapters 6-8). (C&O Ry. C&O Hist. Society Collection)

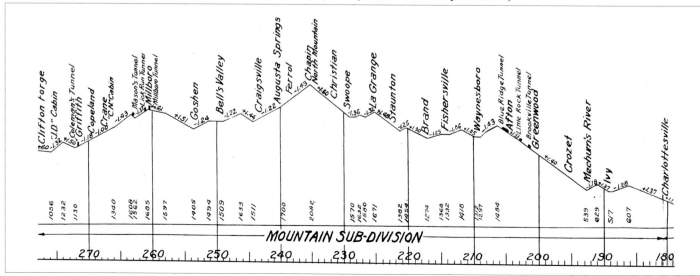

MOUNTAIN SUB-DIVISION

Dist. from Ft. Monroe	Tel. Calls	Station No.	Code No.	STATIONS
181.4	*MO	181	0301	①Charlottesville___Va
182.3	*JC	182	0302	④Union Station___Va
			0300	Baggage_____
			0303	University of Virginia_____
185.7		186	0503	Farmington_____Va
188.9	VY	189	0505	Ivy_____Va
190.8		191	0506	†Oakland_____Va
191.9		192	0507	Mechum's River_Va
194.8	*ZX	195	0509	④Crozet_____Va
197.8		198	0510	Jarman Gap_____Va
199.5	DG	199	0512	④Greenwood_____Va
203.9	AF	204	0515	Afton_____Va
207.8	*BS	208	0518	①④Waynesboro Union Station___Va
208.2		209	0519	Waynesboro_____Va
213.5	FR	214	0521	Fishersville_____Va
217.5		218	0523	††Brand_____Va
218.7		219	0524	‡Peyton_____Va
220.9	*HD	221	0525	①④Staunton_____Va
			0526	Staunton Tkt. Office
224.3		224	0528	La Grange_____Va
225.2		225	0529	†Snyder_____Va
228.8	WO	229	0531	Swoope_____Va
230.8	CF	231	0533	Christian_____Va
234.0		234	0537	North Mountain_Va
234.9		235	0539	Chapin_____Va
237.8		238	0543	Ferrol_____Va
239.6		240	0545	Augusta Springs__Va
242.9		243	0548	Fordwick_____Va
243.9	*CI	244	0550	Craigsville_____Va
248.9		249	0553	Bell's Valley_____Va
252.9	GO	253	0556	④Goshen_____Va
259.9	MB	260	0563	④Milboro_____Va
266.2		266	0565	Crane_____Va
268.1		268	0567	†Copeland_____Va
270.2		270	0569	Griffith_____Va
274.1		274	0571	Longdale_____Va
276.1	*JD			J. D. Cabin_____Va
277.1	*F	277	0577	②④Clifton Forge__Va
			0578	Ticket Office_____
	*F			Sup't Office_____
	*DE			Dispatcher's Office_

*–Day and Night Telegraph Offices.
†–No Siding.
††–Passing Siding only.
‡–Private Siding only.
①–Junction with connecting lines.
②–Junction of Sub-division shown elsewhere.
④–Coupon Stations.

The Commonwealth put Claudius Crozet in charge of the engineering work for the Blue Ridge Railroad. At the time he was the state's Principal Engineer, in charge of projects for the state government. He was an immigrant from France who had been with Napoleon's army when it marched on Moscow in 1812, served as an instructor at the USMA at West Point, and served as an army engineer. His life and work has been the subject of much historical writing. Crozet prepared canal, stagecoach, highway, and railroad maps and did highway surveys as part of his work for the state, but is today most remembered for the Blue Ridge Tunnel. In addition to the long tunnel at the summit, Crozet bored Greenwood, Brookville, and Little Tunnel on the eastern ascent of the mountain. Today Greenwood and Brookville are gone, with the 100-foot-long Little Tunnel still in place.

The Blue Ridge Tunnel's 4,263 foot length, and the unstable earth through which it had to pass, created major problems. It was one of the longest tunnels attempted up to that time, and for years was considered a great engineering feat. The three other tunnels and the track on each side of the summit tunnel were completed by 1854, but Blue Ridge Tunnel would not finally see its first train until 1857. Because of this, the railroad used a temporary track over and around the tunnel construction area. Obviously this entailed very heavy grades, and as a result of having a single locomotive carry no more than 2 or 3 cars at a time, was a major bottleneck until the tunnel could be completed.

One of the innovations employed was that the tunnel was built from both ends at the same time. Crozet made precise calculations, and as a result, the two work forces met on a perfect alignment.

The grade on the east slope ascending the mountain was 1.44% and 1.33%. The west slope grade was 1.23%. Though steep, these represented a very good crossing of this important barrier.

Once complete, the Blue Ridge Railroad was turned over to the Virginia Central for operation, and thus the line was finished between Richmond and Jackson's River.

While Crozet was building across the Blue Ridge, Virginia Central's construction engineer, C. R. Mason (the same man who had been involved with the first work of the Louisa in 1838) was pushing the line over Little North Mountain through a gap discovered by another locating engineer, Charles Ellet. He had helped in locating the JR&K Canal in earlier years. H. D. Whitcomb was his assistant. Whitcomb would be prominent in building the C&O across West Virginia in the early 1870s.

The biggest effort was building up the North Mountain grade, which entailed several tunnels, Millboro (1,335 ft.), Lick Run (290 ft.) and Mason's (326 ft) on the east slope and Coleman's (368 ft) on the western. The biggest problem was Millboro Tunnel, and more importantly the large fill that was necessary just to the west of the tunnel. It was by far the biggest earth moving project that the Virginia Central ever undertook, and required another temporary track around it until it could be completed. This temporary track wasn't removed until the mid-1870s, and was a troublesome operating impediment until the fill was finished.

West of the Blue Ridge the towns of Waynesboro and Staunton were reached, both of which would prove to be large suppliers of a traffic of mainly agricultural products in the decades to come as well as small industrial output. Ascending North Mountain and in to Clifton Forge, the countryside was isolated and very rural, with no large towns encountered. Millboro, Goshen, and Craigsville were the most prominent towns and stations.

In the ensuing years, Mason's and Coleman's tunnels were bypassed and taken out of service (1946-1948), leaving today on the entire line from Charlottesville to Clifton Forge only Little, Blue Ridge, Millboro, and Lick Run tunnels in use.

Construction stopped once the line reached Jackson's River Station, in what is now the town of Selma, just west of Clifton Forge. This became the end terminal of the Virginia Central, though it was to have gone on an additional eight miles to the town of Covington. At that point the state-sponsored Covington and Ohio was to have been built to the Ohio, connecting with the Virginia Central. As with the Blue Ridge Railroad, it was probably planned that the Covington & Ohio would be leased to Virginal Central in a similar manner. However, lack of funds stymied the Virginia Central, and the Commonwealth was slow in building the Covington and Ohio. As a result, the War Between the States intervened. Following the

war Virginia Central and Covington & Ohio were merged under the name Chesapeake & Ohio in 1868.

Virginia Central's terminal at Jackson's River consisted of a freight and a passenger depot, a turntable and a siding. A hotel and a few other buildings clustered around it. It was near the location of the still extant Oakland Church.

After Millboro fill was finished the line was complete and was operated in that way until the 1920s. It was in 1943 that Greenwood Tunnel was bypassed and sealed. One can still see the elaborate eastern portal of the abandoned tunnel with its parabolic brick portal as originally designed by Crozet. When Interstate 64 was built in the 1970s Brookville (originally "Brooksville") Tunnel was delighted and a temporary track used until construction was complete. In 1942 a new Blue Ridge Tunnel was completed after several years of work. The new tunnel was on a lower gradient and different alignment from the Crozet tunnel. The old tunnel was left in place, and today is the center of a movement to create a hiking/biking trail to its western portal, which is another brick and stone construction with the characteristic parabolic design.

Early traffic on the line consisted of passenger and general freight trains. Coal became steadily more important as C&O established its traffic from the West Virginia fields to the sea at Newport News, therefore more coal trains had to travel over the saw-tooth profile of the Mountain Subdivision, ascending some very steep grades eastbound. This problem was solved in 1890 when the Richmond & Alleghany Railroad, running along the James Riv-

Although it is not as well known today, C&O did use the H-7 class simple articulated 2-8-8-2s on the Mountain Subdivision. The engineers didn't like them because of very close tunnel clearances. One engineer said that he sometimes thought that his H-7 was about to launch into the air on some of the vertical curves. Here H-7 No. 1551 is headed west from Charlottesville with manifest freight. (TLC Collection)

In the high days of C&O's passenger service, J-3 4-8-4 Greenbrier No. 602 powers The Sportsman near Charlottesville on September 7, 1936, looking just as it did when it came from Lima the year before with centered headlight and high bell. This very patrician appearance was fitting for "George Washington's Railroad." Heavy Pacifics and Mountain types controlled the Charlottesville-Clifton Forge-Hinton grades until 1935 when the five 4-8-4s arrived to take on the heaviest trains. (Harold Vollrath Collection)

er (see Chapters 6-8) was acquired. Most coal then went via that line, and the Mountain Subdivision was left to handle passenger trains, fast freights, and local business. The through passenger trains and fast freights became more important after 1889 when C&O acquired trackage rights over the Virginia Midland (later Southern, now NS) east of Orange, giving it access to Washington and the connections to the great Northeastern railway systems.

In the middle decades of the 20th Century, the Mountain Subdivision had settled into its role as a largely passenger line. Local commodities were mainly the products of forest and farm. Connections were made with the B&O's Valley Line at Staunton, and considerable interchange occurred there until the B&O abandoned that line. At Basic City, just to the east of Waynesboro (later merged into a single city), C&O crossed the Norfolk & Western's Shenandoah Valley Subdivision, and effected a large interchange business there.

A large cement plant was located at Fordwick, near Craigsville, which supplied huge amounts of traffic until its closure in the 1970s. Iron business was important in this region and there were several iron furnaces that were served by C&O. Victoria Furnace was located a few miles away from Goshen and was reached by a narrow gauge railroad. At Longdale, the Mountain Subdivision was

intersected by another narrow gauge line, serving the Longdale Iron Company's furnace, about 6 miles away. By the early years of the 20th Century these operations, along with others closed down.

After World War II C&O undertook a huge improvement project on the Mountain Subdivision which entailed the bypassing of Mason's, Greenwood, and Coleman's Tunnels and the elimination of many sharp curves, resulting in much better operational conditions. The engineering of the mid-20th Century replaced the engineering of the mid-19th! The project was expensive and undertaken over several years. One of the reasons for the massive project was to improve the right of way for new passenger service that C&O's chairman, Robert R. Young, wanted. It also improved operating conditions for regular passenger trains and freight as well.

In the 1960s the Mountain Subdivision began to lose importance because of the steady decline in passenger service and elimination of trains. As the fast freight business also declined, and local business dried up, the Mountain was left with much less traffic that it once had. By the mid-1980s CSX was considering abandoning portions of the line (along with the Piedmont Subdivision), but it was kept, and used to take empty coal trains west. The process that was used was to take the heavy loaded trains down the easy grades of the James River line to Richmond and on to Newport

News, then the empties were brought back over the Piedmont and Mountain lines. Since both lines were single track this helped eliminate traffic congestion.

In 2004 the Buckingham Branch Railroad, a short line which bought C&O's Buckingham Branch (see Chapter 8), leased the Piedmont and Mountain Subdivisions from CSX and operates the line now. The Mountain Subdivision is still (as of 2011) used by passenger trains, as Amtrak's *Cardinal* passes over the line each way three times per week. CSX still moves most of its westbound empty coal trains over this line by trackage rights, and Buckingham Branch operates its own local freights successfully.

Motive Power on the Mountain Subdivision followed the development of the passenger trains closely, since by the time that the C&O began to buy bigger and more powerful locomotives, the heaviest of its business, the coal trade, had been diverted away from the Mountain Subdivision. Small 4-4-0s and 4-6-0s handled the through passenger trains over this line up until 1902, when the first of the new heavier passenger engines arrived on the scene. In 1902 C&O purchased the first of its 4-6-2 types. This wheel arrangement had not been used in regular service by American railroads up until this time. C&O wanted a more powerful locomotives specifically for its heavy mountain grades, so the 4-6-2 was designed. At the same time the Missouri Pacific was doing the same thing, and both roads received their 4-6-2s at about the same time. MoPac called its engine a "Pacific" type, and C&O dubbed its a "Mountain Type." But, because the MoPac's locomotive re-

ceived more attention in the trade press and sooner, the name Pacific became the universal appellation for the 4-6-2 wheel arrangement, and C&O was content to call its engines Pacifics as well. At the same time the 4-4-0 type was enlarged into the 4-4-2 Atlantic type, and these handled the light 6-9 wooden cars that constituted most C&O trains of the era.

In 1911 C&O designed yet another new wheel arrangement, which enlarged the Pacific type in power: the 4-8-2. C&O again used the name "Mountain" for this new locomotive. The name stuck. On most railroads where this new locomotive became popular the name Mountain was standard. By this time C&O's passenger trains were longer, with bigger, heavier cars, and steel cars were soon the order of the day, making the big Mountains important. Heavier and more powerful 4-6-2s also arrived through 1926, and by the mid-1920s the standard power west from Charlottesville and east from Clifton Forge was a Mountain, or a couple of heavy Pacifics doubleheading, or a combination of the two.

Another innovation occurred in 1935 when C&O recieved from Lima Locomotive Works an example of its "Super Power" locomotive design in the form of the 4-8-4 type. Known as "Northern" type, on most railroads, C&O called them "Greenbriers." The giant new engines, Nos. 600-604, could handle a 13 heavyweight cars train over the Mountain Subdivision, and a second engine (either a Mountain or a heavy Pacific) was needed if the train exceeded that limit. The Greenbriers were largely captive to the Charlottesville-Clifton Forge-Hinton operations their whole

After dieselization, sets of four or five GP7s and GP9s were common on Mountain Subdivision freights. Here GP9 No. 6222 followed by GP7 5878 and three other units are on a coal train eastbound near Crozet, having just come off the Blue Ridge grade in September 1959. The reason for a coal train in this locale isn't usual unless there was a problem the river line or the coal was headed to Potomac yard for use in the Washington area. (C&O Ry. Photo, C&O Hist. Soc. Coll., CSPR-4580)

In another photo featuring a 4-8-4, this time J-3a No. 610 is seen powering Train No. 4/46, The Sportsman, as it emerges from Brookville Tunnel near Greenwood, Va., on the eastern slope of the Blue Ridge in July 1948. The locomotive is brand new, one of five built by Lima Locomotive Works for C&O in May and June 1948, the last new passenger steamers in the U. S. except for N&W's last three J-class 4-8-4s built in 1950. The tunnel is now gone, as I-64 crosses this scene. (J. I. Kelly Photo, C&O Hist. Soc. Collection, COHS-42)

lives. In 1942 two more 4-8-4s arrived (Nos. 605-606) and in 1948 five additional engines were added to the 4-8-4 fleet (J-3A Nos. 610-614). In 1951 the EMD E8 diesels arrived and by early the following year steam was gone from C&O passenger trains.

In freight service up through the early years of the 20th Century the 4-6-0s and 2-8-0 types were the most common on the Mountain SD, but 2-8-2 Mikado types began to be used in the middle-'teens, and more so after the ultra-modern K-2,3,3a class Mikados came in the early 1920s. The Compound 2-6-6-2s, which became popular on C&O in the 1911-1925 era, also saw service on Mountain SD freights. The 2-10-2 types inherited from merged railroads, were also used on this line, as were the giant H-7 2-8-8-2 simple articulated types. It was said that the H-7's stack cleared the roof of Millboro Tunnel by only a few inches, and that the blast of its exhaust would dislodge bricks and throw them back toward the cab. After 1942 when the K-4 class 2-8-4's arrived they became the common power for the trough manifest fast freights.

In the diesel era the ever-present GP7s and GP9s ruled on the Mountain Subdivision, supplanted by second generation diesels starting in about 1970. CSX's westbound coal trains today use a pair of the giant GE or EMD high-horsepower units Buckingham Branch uses a variety of second-hand units for its local work.

Charlottesville, the eastern terminal of the Mountain Subdivision had a small yard, engine terminal, roundhouse, coaling and water stations, and full terminal facilities (see Chapter 5). One of the major operations at Charlottesville was to adjust the consists of mainline named passenger trains. The system worked in this way: C&O trains started at Cincinnati and at Louisville and met at Ashland, Kentucky, where the through cars from each were put together into one larger train. This train then moved over the mainline to Charlottesville. Here it was broken up with through cars for Washington and points east placed on one train and cars for Richmond and Newport News on a second. These trains would then leave Charlottesville about 30 minutes apart, and go their respective ways at Gordonsville. Coming west the operation reversed with trains combined at Charlottesville and broken at Ashland. This required a coach yard at Charlottesville to accommodate passenger cars of various types that terminated here, or held for other trains. A branch of the C&O commissary was also located here because dining cars were often rotated among trains at this point or were provisioned en route from this point. This operation continued through the end of C&O passenger operations, and for a few years into Amtrak operation, until the Richmond-Newport News sections of the trains were discontinued. C&O's operations in Charlottesville were centered around its large Georgian Revival columned depot on Main Street. The yard and engine facilities were located immediately east of this location.

C&O passenger trains also stopped at Charlottesville Union Station, which was located in the wye formed by the crossing of C&O and Southern mainlines 9/10th of a mile west of the C&O station. This station was particularly convenient to passengers to and from the University of Virginia campus. Today Amtrak's *Cardinal* uses the old Union Station for its trains on both C&O and Norfolk Southern (old SR mainline). The C&O depot was sold and now houses offices. The most of the yard and all the engine service facilities are gone. (See also Chapter 12 for passenger details.)

Statistics (as of 1948)

Mileage: 95.7 miles

Stations: 25 names locations.

Branches: None

Connections: N&W at Waynesboro; Southern at Charlottesville; Chesapeake Western at Staunton; (B&O at Staunton until that line was sold).

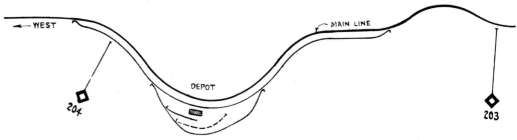

Track layout at Afton featured several sidings, which served the freight station as house and team tracks. Afton was a small shipping center for framers in the region. (C&O Historical Society Collection)

In a later day, three EMD E8s power No. 4 as it passes the little Afton depot near the top of the Blue Ridge grade in about 1960, with 13 cars in consist, including two mail storage, a full RPO, express and baggage, plus coaches, sleepers, and a business car bringing up the rear. (W. E. Warden, Jr. Photo)

Three GP9s and GP7s, led by 6246, bring an extra freight west near Afton in about 1957, including three box cars and empty hoppers. (C&O Ry. Photo, C&O Hist. Society Collection, CSPR-4581)

Probably the most famous feature on the Mountain Subdivision mainline was Blue Ridge Tunnel, a real engineering wonder when Claudius Crozet bored it in 1854-1857. This is a photo of the west portal of this tunnel, with the parabolic shape that was characteristic of the of the four tunnels Crozet had to use on the Blue Ridge Railroad. It was in service until a new tunnel was bored in 1940-42. This portal is to serve as the destination point of a bike-hike trail that is proposed. (TLC Collection)

Emerging from the new Blue Ridge Tunnel, J-3A 4-8-4 No. 614 has No. 5/47, the westbound Sportsman in tow on July 15, 1948. No. 614 would be saved by C&O and placed in the B&O Museum, from which it was taken to power the Chessie Safety Express of 1979-81, and later other trips by Ross Rowland. As of this writing (2011) it is on display at the C&O Heritage Center, Clifton Forge, Va. - The Greenbriers could handle any train with up to 13 cars. If the consist was heavier, then double heading was required, which could mean two 4-8-4s or a 4-8-4 and a 4-8-2. (J. I. Kelly photo, D. Wallace Johnson Collection)

Waynesboro Union Station was located where C&O crossed over the Norfolk & Western's Shenandoah Valley Line (Roanoke-Hagerstown, Md.) The elevator, in center background, led down to a shed on the N&W tracks below. This station was originally built in 1890 and was called Basic. Waynesboro had its own station about a mile west of this point, but C&O decided to make this the main stop for the two towns because of its location at the N&W crossing, and the other station was downgraded to local freight business. The two towns eventually merged into what is today Waynesboro. (C&O Historical Society Collection)

The large passenger station at Staunton was fitting this principal city on the Mountain Subdivision between Charlottesville and Clifton Forge. It was built in 1906. The freight station is barely visible to the immediate right. This, obviously, is from a ca. 1915 postcard view. The station is very much in existence today and is used as a restaurant. (TLC Collection)

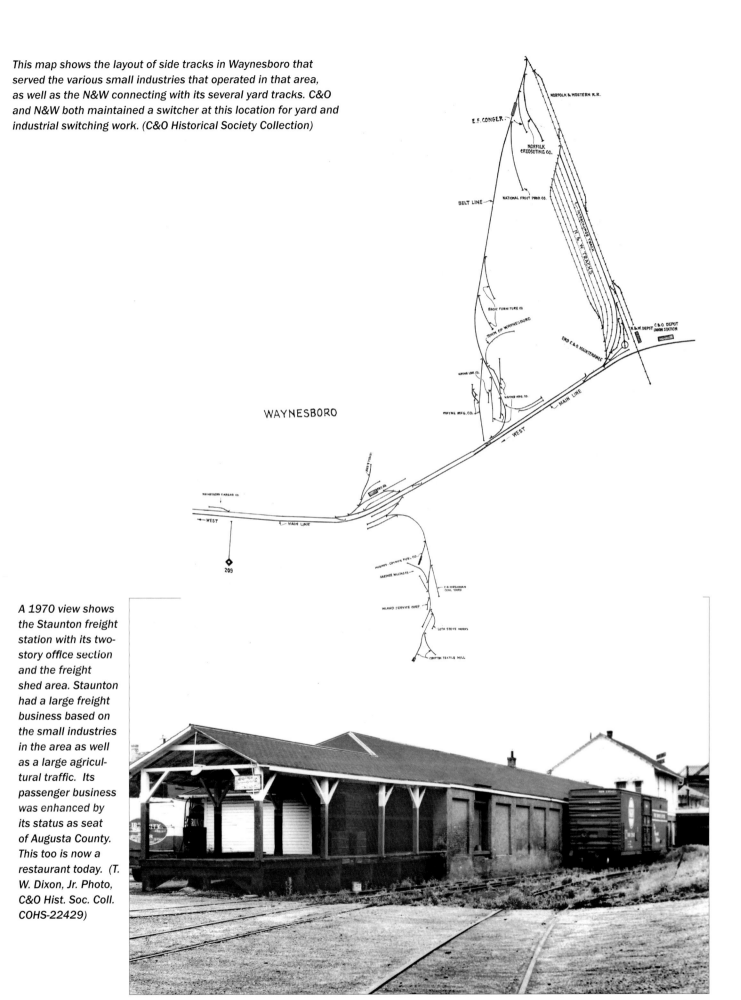

This map shows the layout of side tracks in Waynesboro that served the various small industries that operated in that area, as well as the N&W connecting with its several yard tracks. C&O and N&W both maintained a switcher at this location for yard and industrial switching work. (C&O Historical Society Collection)

WAYNESBORO

A 1970 view shows the Staunton freight station with its two-story office section and the freight shed area. Staunton had a large freight business based on the small industries in the area as well as a large agricultural traffic. Its passenger business was enhanced by its status as seat of Augusta County. This too is now a restaurant today. (T. W. Dixon, Jr. Photo, C&O Hist. Soc. Coll. COHS-22429)

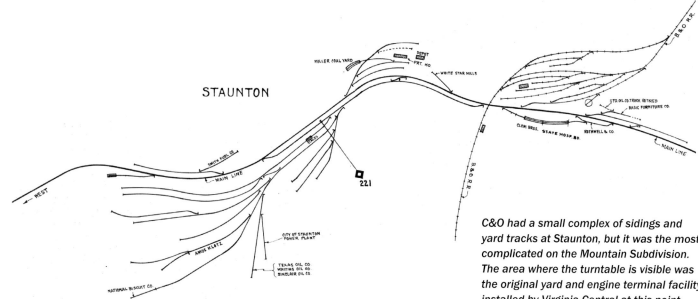

STAUNTON

C&O had a small complex of sidings and yard tracks at Staunton, but it was the most complicated on the Mountain Subdivision. The area where the turntable is visible was the original yard and engine terminal facility installed by Virginia Central at this point in the mid-1850s. It was an operational division point until the late 1870s. By the 20th Century this area was used for general freight for the city. It should noted that Staunton was the junction point with the Baltimore & Ohio's Shenandoah Valley line and there was a good deal of interchange traffic here until the 1942 sale of that line to Chesapeake Western. (C&O Historical Society Collection)

On the steep ascent to the top of Ellet's Gap on Little North Mountain, C&O required several tunnels. This view shows the brick portal of Millboro Tunnel, near the town by that name. At 1,335 feet, it wasn't a large effort, but the huge earthen fill that was required just to the west of it was. (Aubrey Wiley Photo)

This evocative publicity photo was used by C&O one many of its passenger ads and brochures, as boys wave to a passenger train powered by J-3A No. 610 in about 1950 near Goshen. (C&O Historical Society Collection)

After the track was relocated in 1947, C&O replaced the old Goshen station with this modern looking cinder-block structure which served the town to the end of passenger service, seen here in 1971. This building is still in use, by the Buckingham Branch Railroad which leases and operates the line. (T. W. Dixon, Jr. photo, C&O Hist. Soc. Collection)

The east portal of Lick Run Tunnel (only 290 feet), just west of Millboro was interesting in that its portal was of ashlar stone. It was between Millboro and Lick Run tunnels that a large fill required use of temporary tracks until the mid-1870s, though the work was begun in the 1850s. (Aubrey Wiley Photo)

A typical No. 4, The Sportsman, is seen here using a recently relocated track near Millboro (note the old route at left) on May 10, 1951. The 14-car train was about normal for the time, mixed between heavyweight cars in the green paint scheme and new lightweight cars in the three-color scheme. J-3a No. 612 is the power. A large line-improvement program rebuilt and realigned a large portion of the Mountain Subdivision 1946-1948 which eased curves, bypassed Mason's and Coleman's tunnels, and improved operating conditions over the original line built in the 1850s.(Robert F. Collins Photo, TLC Collection)

Santa Fe type 2-10-2s were often use on the Mountain Subdivision. Here a local freight is seen at North Mountain with B-1 class No. 2959 and the usual second caboose. (C&O Ry. Photo, C&O Hist. Society Collection, CSPR-2352 & 2353)

A C&O official photo shows the track realignment program in progress. The new track is being built to the right as the hill is cut down. Mason's Tunnel, seen at left, will be eliminated by the cut that the equipment is working on. The view is from September 1946. (C&O Ry. Photo, C&O Hist. Society Collection, CSPR-57.193)

The Mountain Subdivision's western terminus was at JD Cabin where it entered the eastern yard limits at Clifton Forge. In this October 1956 view No. 5/47, the westbound Sportsman is just coming off the Mountain line. On the Jackson River bridge to the right, a local train from the Craig Valley Branch is waiting on the James River Subdivision mainline. It will enter the yard after No. 5 passes. JD Cabin is just out of the photo at right. (C&O Ry. Photo, C&O Hist. Society Collection, CSPR-10393.392)

10: Clifton Forge

This chapter deals with one of C&O's two largest installations in Virginia, Clifton Forge, which served as its secondary system-wide shop, and principal classification yard for eastbound coal.

The name Clifton Forge first appears in prominence on the C&O in 1889, when the new management of the company made a complete reorganization of the line, installed new yards and shops, and rebuilt the property in general. Before this the town on the C&O in this area was called Williamson's, and before that Jackson's River Station was the station for this region. The Clifton Forge itself, an antebellum iron furnace and forge, was located a few miles to the east along the Jackson River.

The Virginia Central arrived in what is now the Clifton Forge area in 1857 when its rails reached Jackson's River Station. This was located in what is now the unincorporated town of Selma, just to the west of present-day Clifton Forge, near the old Oakland Church. It had a simple frame station, turntable, two sidings, and a hotel. The stage coaches headed to and from the Springs and along the old James River & Kanawha Turnpike to the Ohio met the trains at this point. The intention was to build Virginia Central tracks about nine more miles to Covington, but lack of funds stopped them here, then the War Between the States intervened.

By the early 1870s, after C&O had built its western extension to the Ohio it was necessary to have some type of location where trains could stop for fuel, water and crew changes on the line between Staunton and Hinton, and this was selected. As a result, a town grew up around the C&O's station, small yard, and roundhouse near Smith Creek, within what is now the center of Clifton Forge. The station and post office used the name Williamson's.

In 1881 the Richmond & Alleghany Railway was built along the old JR&K Canal from Richmond through Lynchburg to Williamson's, crossing the river near what is now the US Rt. 220 bridge, and entering the C&O yard at that point. The C&O's station and offices were located along the Jackson River's bank. The station was in a large frame hotel building, and dispatchers and other offices were in nondescript structures nearby. The main street of the town was the C&O main line. Across the track were the roundhouse, shop, and yard tracks. This is about where the C&O Heritage Center railway museum is now located.

Williamson's remained as a small divisional point and crew change point until 1889-90, when the new Ingalls management undertook a complete rebuilding and reorganization of the C&O. They decided to establish a major shop and yard facility here. To do so they purchased a large amount of land west of the town, which was laid out in residential and business lots, and was sold to raise money for building the new shops and yards here. At the same time the town's name was changed to Clifton Forge. West Clifton Forge was the location of the shops.

Track diagram chart showing arrangement of yard tracks in Clifton Forge. As can be seen the area covered was over four miles long. (C&O Historical Society Collection)

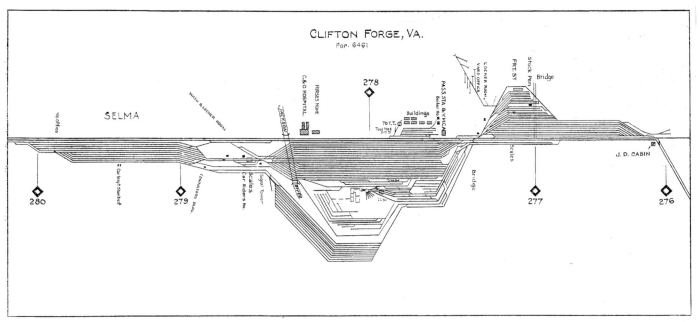

During the next couple of yards a large shop facility was built and many long yard tracks placed. The yard became the repair facility for locomotive operating east of Hinton (as Huntington, W. Va. shops serviced locomotives west of Hinton). The yard was used mainly for classification of coal loads headed to Newport News, which was steadily growing in this era.

By the mid-1890s the eastbound coal traffic had become a torrent, as almost 1,000 cars per day arrived at Clifton Forge. Trackage was steadily expanded and a new yard was placed to the west of the old Williamson's (Smith Creek) area.

As the modern configuration of the C&O emerged following the World War I era, Clifton Forge became the main pivot of the line's eastern operations. The Clifton Forge Division included the James River Subdivision to Gladstone, the Mountain Subdivision to Charlottesville, and the Alleghany Subdivision to Hinton, as well as the branches associated with these lines of road. A big hotel building was erected near the old Williamson's location with the passenger station in its lower floor, and beside it a large Railroad YMCA building was erected for use by crews always from their home terminal in the 1893-96 period. In 1905 a large division office building was placed beside them (it is still in use as CSX main office in the town today).

In 1923-26 the yard was greatly expanded, and an all new yard built at Selma, to the west of the shops. The main yard was expanded, and the shops were also modernized and expanded. By this time over 1,000 people were employed in the shops and about that many in train service, making Clifton Forge topmost in C&O operations in Virginia, though the Newport

News yards were larger in trackage and area. The facilities remained in this configuration and degree of development until the end of the steam era, with a decrease in activity in the early 1930s and an increase in work and activity during the World War II years.

With the coming of diesels, the employment in the shops steadily declined. In 1955 a new diesel shop was built over part of the old steam erecting shop and maintenance work continued here, but not nearly the old force of men was required for diesel maintenance. Car shops continued to work on cars with running repairs (repair in place).

In the old Williamson's area, where the original 1870s roundhouse had been the Smith Creek yard was built in the mid-1890s, and a large LCL freight station area with attendant trackage was built. This served as a loading and trans-loading station for LCL freight not only from the region but from all the subdivisions that centered here. This large operation as in steady decline following WWII as motor freight and package delivery companies took away much of the railways' LCL freight business. The station's operation ended about the same time C&O discontinued its LCL operations in about 1962.

A large icing platform was placed opposite the passenger station area for re-icing refrigerator cars en route over the system. It was in service until the late 1960s by which time mechanical refrigerator cars had replaced ice-cooled cars.

In the mid-20th Century configuration coal trains headed into Clifton Forge were staged at Selma, and put over the hump yard into the main yard where eastbound coal trains were made up for Newport

GP9 6045 leads two other units on an eastbound coal train passing through Smith Creek yard and about to take the James River Subdivision toward Gladstone, Richmond, and Newport News, in 1956. This is the east throat of Clifton Forge yard complex at a location called JD Cabin. (C&O Ry. Photo, C&O Historical Society Collection, CSPR-10393.162)

News. Coal was classified in the hump yard based on what ships it was to be dumped into at Newport News. The main yard was used for this, as well as classification of manifest freight, while the Smith Creek yard on the eastern side of the town was used to stage incoming manifest freight from the east and to prepare eastbound freight trains.

One unusual aspect of C&O operations at Clifton Forge was that beginning in 1896 the company established a hospital for employees. In those days hospitals were few and far between in this region, and C&O wanted to give its employees good care, so an employees' hospital association was set up whereby a very small amount was deducted from pay to keep the hospital in operation. First, it at first housed in a hotel building near the shops that was available when C&O moved its hotel operation to the center of town over the passenger station. In 1917 a new brick building replaced the old one, and in the 1950s a modern addition expanded it. It was later sold and is now Alleghany Regional Hospital in Low Moor, just west of the old location, and the old hospital was subsumed into a high-rise senior center there today. The C&O had only one other hospital, at Huntington, W. Va., but the Clifton Forge facility was the princi-

This 1947 photo looking west toward the main facilities at Clifton Forge (C&O Ry. Photo, C&O Historical Society Collection, CSPR-2332):

1 - Passenger Station and Railroad YMCA

2 - Division Office Building

3 - Railway Express Building

4 - Streamlined Coaling Station

5 - Re-icing platform

6 - Company housing

7 - Less than Carload Freight station and loading/transfer station

8 - LCL ("Package") Box cars parked so that their doors are aligned so that freight can be moved car-to-car

9 - Stock pens and chutes

10 - Smith Creek Yard (Manifest freight)

11 - Main Lines

12 - Main yard (Coal classification)

pal one, with a famous school of nursing attached.

As operations declined during the 1960s and 1970s, employment at Clifton Forge decreased. In 1982 the shops were assigned to maintain General Electric locomotives for the system, but then in about 1992 they were closed entirely with operations moving to Huntington and the former B&O shop at Cumberland, Md. During this period the Smith Creek yard was taken up, the main yard had many tracks eliminated, and the Selma yard across the Jackson river was taken out. In the 1990s a new high-tech fueling facility was installed in the area that used to be occupied by the coach yard west of the station area, and a new turntable installed at that point, which resulted in abandonment of all the ready track facilities on the opposite of the yard east of the shops. Today CSX uses the old division office building for its operating personnel, and the fueling pad is the center of activity. The main yard is used for switching as needed. Coal and grain trains are the principal business.

H-8s 1600 and 1617 at Smith Creek yard in September 1947. No. 1617 is leaving westbound with a manifest freight. Clifton Forge was the center of operations for many of the H-8s. (C. H. Kerrigan Photo)

The large Railroad YMCA and passenger station (first floor) that served Clifton Forge for so long. It was built in 1896 as the station/hotel, but when the YMCA that was beside it was torn down in 1923, the hotel rooms became the YMCA. It lasted until 1975. The coach yard is at left with a Pullman visible. It was almost always filled with C&O, NYC, PRR and Pullman cars that constantly brought special parties to the Homestead or Greenbrier resorts. The combination car on the track opposite the platform was used on the trains to Hot Springs that ferried the sleepers up and back from the mainline trains which left them or picked them up here. (C&O Ry. Photo, C&O Historical Society Collection, CSPR-10393.171)

K-4 2-8-4 No. 2765 is about to leave Clifton Forge eastbound with No. 4, The Sportsman, for Charlottesville at 7:15 a. m. May 11, 1946, while the motor train that will later leave down the James River Line is parked at the left. Before the new Hudsons and Greenbriers arrived in 1948 K-4s that were equipped for passenger service were often seen on passenger trains. They were about as powerful as a J-2 or J-3. (Bruce Fales Photo, Jay Williams Collection)

The streamlined coaling station was built at Clifton Forge specially to fuel the giant M-1 class steam-turbine-electric locomotive that were bought to haul the new Chessie train. When the train was cancelled the 3 locomotives were used in regular passenger service for a year and then scrapped. Here the first one, No. 500, is being coaled for its maiden run out of Clifton Forge in December 1947. (C&O Ry. Photo, C&O Historical Society Collection, CSPR-1326)

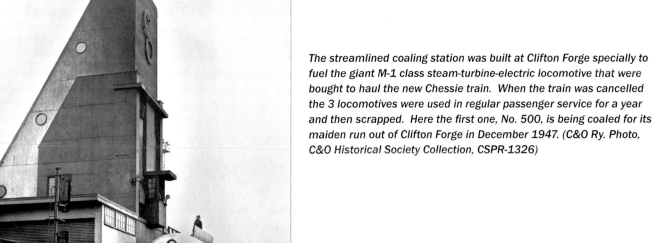

The tracks around the defunct streamlined coaling station were used to stage GP7 and GP9 diesels as the C&O dieselized Clifton Forge operations. The ready tracks were being converted from steam use in this July 1957 scene. (C&O Ry. Photo, C&O Historical Society Collection, CSPR-10469.846)

In March 1949 before the arrival of the first diesel, the Clifton Forge ready tracks were a busy place. Looking east from the coaling station. Note the big depot/hotel in the left background. Both large and small power is gathering here for service. (C&O Ry. Photo, C&O Historical Society Collection, CSPR-2325)

Aerial view of the Clifton Forge shops at the height of their operations:

1 - Roundhouse (two different buildings)

2 - Radial tracks and second turntable

3 - Stores department building

4 - Erecting shop

5 - Tender shop, machine shop, blacksmith shop

6 - Repair In place tracks for car work

7 - Materials yard

8 - Bridge from Selma yard across the river (receiving yard for coal)

9 - Main yard

10 - Power House

A variety of steam power at the Clifton Forge roundhouse in March 1949 includes F-15 light Pacific No. 449, G-7 Consolidation No. 793, K-2 Mikado and others. (C&O Ry. Photo, C&O Historical Society Collection, CSPR-2330)

The new diesel shop was simply superimposed over a portion of the steam shop when it was installed in 1955. Here units are seen exiting the façade of the modernistic building right after its construction 1955. C&O Ry. Photo, C&O Historical Society Collection, CSPR-10246.97)

Diesel repairs taking place in the new diesel shop at Clifton Forge in 1955. Maintenance of diesels was much simpler than steam and the shop forces were drastically reduced as a result. (C&O Ry. Photo, C&O Historical Society Collection, CSPR-10246.119)

The Clifton Forge roundhouse as it appeared at the end of its life, with just a single GP9 present in this 1956 view. The yard was clogged with coal in various grades awaiting trains to take it to Newport News. (C&O Ry. Photo, C&O Historical Society Collection, CSPR-10393.387)

Aerial view of the whole Clifton Forge Shop area in 1956:

1 - Old shop buildings

2 - New diesel shop

3 - Coaling station

4 - Cinder conveyor

5 - Ready tracks

6 - Stores building and car repair tracks

7 - Bridge to Selma yard cross Jackson River

8 - Coal receiving yard (Selma yard)

9 - Extension of Selma yard

10 - Beginning of hump yard

C&O Hospital at Clifton Forge as it looked soon after the new brick buildling was erected in 1917. (C&O Historical Society Collection)

The Alleghany Subdivision runs 77.8 miles from Clifton Forge, Virginia to Hinton, West Virginia. Of that distance 30 miles is within the Commonwealth of Virginia, running from Clifton Forge to a point inside Alleghany Tunnel, at Alleghany. This chapter will cover that 30 miles. The balance of the Alleghany Subdivision has been covered in the book West Virginia Railroads, Vol. 2, Chesapeake & Ohio *by this author.*

The Alleghany Subdivision was built between 1867 and 1872. The first 12 miles, between Clifton Forge and Covington was completed in 1867. The next segment of 23 miles to White Sulphur Springs, about 5 miles west of the state line, was opened on July 1, 1869. The rest of the line was completed to Hinton in 1872, as part of the extension of the C&O to the Ohio River across the new state of West Virginia.

No additions were made to the line from 1857, when the Virginia Central tracks arrived at Jackson's River Station not far from the present Low Moor, at the western end of the Clifton Forge yard, until after the War Between the States. It was only after the war that the company was able to build the 12.6 miles into Covington, reaching that point July 31, 1867. In 1868 Virginia Central and Covington & Ohio were merged to form Chesapeake & Ohio after C. P. Huntington became president and principal backer in 1869. One of his first moves was to complete the line from Covington to White Sulphur Springs, which was already under way, using grading and tunnel work that had been accomplished by Covington & Ohio before the war. Up until that time stagecoaches met the trains at Jackson's River (then Covington) taking people on to the "Grand Hotel" at White Sulphur Springs. Huntington wanted to capitalize quickly on the "Springs trade," a feature of C&O passenger business until the end.

The main work on the Alleghany Subdivision in Virginia was the ascent of Alleghany Mountain [Alleghany is spelled with an "a" instead of an "e" in this part of Virginia]. This entailed several tunnels, and building through a wild and isolated region. Some of the grading and tunnel work had been accomplished by the state-owned Covington & Ohio Railroad before the war. The original concept was for Virginia Central and Covington & Ohio to join at Covington and complete a link to the Ohio. After the war, the rights and property of the Covington & Ohio was given to the new C&O, which also assumed the rights and property of the Virginia Central.

When the line was extended to Covington it appears that Jackson's River Station was abandoned and the Virginia Central's terminal facility was moved east to Williamson's (the small town situated on the western end of present-day Clifton Forge). Williamson's acquired a roundhouse, yard, and station as it began to serves as a division point between Staunton and Hinton in the 1870s.

The road to Covington was easy, with no great geographical barriers as the C&O followed the Jackson River's south bank, crossing it at Steele, just east of Covington, and again just west of the Covington station.

West of Covington, the Alleghany Mountain grade began (see the profile on the next page). The route had been selected and some of the work done on the grading, filling, and tunnels before the war by the Covington and Ohio. The first tunnel west of Covington is Mud Tunnel (originally called Red Hill),

Alleghany Subdivision Station List (1948) showing the entire line in Virginia and West Virginia.

ALLEGHANY SUB-DIVISION

Dist. from Ft. Monroe	Tel. Calls	Station No.	Code No.	STATIONS
277.5	*F	277	0577	④**Clifton Forge**____Va
278.1		278		†H. Y. Cabin_____Va
281.2		281	0730	Low Moor_____Va
286.6		287	0734	†Mallow_____Va
289.7	CD	290	0738	②④**Covington**_____Va
291.2	*BS	291		††B. S. Cabin_____Va
292.1		292	0782	‡Boys Home_____Va
293.4		293	0784	McDowell_____Va
295.3		295	0786	Callaghan_____Va
297.7		298	0788	Moss Run_____Va
300.2		300	0790	Backbone_____Va
304.2		304	0792	Jerry's Run_____Va
306.4	*A	306	0797	④**Alleghany**_____Va
308.0		308	1000	Tuckahoe_____W Va
311.9	*WS	312	1002	④**White Sulphur Springs**____W Va
			1003	" Hotel_____
315.5		315	1008	Hart's Run____W Va
317.3		317	1010	Caldwell_____W Va
319.8		320	1012	②†Whitcomb___W Va
322.8	*RV	323	1014	④**Ronceverte**___W Va
326.5		326	1018	†Rockland_____W Va
329.0		329	1022	④**Fort Spring**___W Va
330.1		330	1024	†Snow Flake____W Va
330.8		331	1026	‡Frazier_____W Va
335.8		336	1030	④**Alderson**_____W Va
336.4	*AD	336½		††A. D. Cabin___W Va
337.4		337	1032	†Glenray_____W Va
339.4		339	1034	Wolf Creek____W Va
341.5		341	1036	†Riffe_____W Va
343.4		343	1038	Pence Spring__W Va
345.3		345	1040	Lowell_____W Va
347.2		347	1042	Talcott_____W Va
349.5	*MW	350	1046	Hilldale_____W Va
352.6		353	1049	Wiggins_____W Va
355.3	*MX	355		M. X. Cabin__W Va

with a length of 634 feet near milepost 294 near the Callaghan station. The next is Moore's (331 feet) and Lake's (712 feet) very close together near MP 301, and then Kelley's (467 feet) at MP 302. The longest was Lewis (4,077 feet) near the top of the grade. All these tunnels were double tracked when C&O installed its second track in the area after the turn of the 20th Century except for Lewis. A new single track bore was made at Lewis in 1932 which was part of C&O's 1920s-30s tunnel expansion program that completed the double tracked line between Clifton Forge and Cincinnati. Other problems on the ascending grade included the need to make some very large fills. The largest of these was across a ravine created by Jerry's Run (a small creek, called a "run" in this region). It required a water tunnel to be dug through the solid rock at the bottom of the declivity, and the largest railroad fill in the world was required to bridge it. A temporary track was built around it, much as had been done at Blue Ridge Tunnel and the Millboro Fill to the east, and a special saddle tank locomotive took one or two cars over the ridge. This, of course, finally ended when the fill was complete about 1873, but not before a passenger car being carried over the temporary track derailed and fell over the fill, killing about 10 people. This would be the worst wreck in C&O history as far as the number of people killed.

Once the track was through Lewis Tunnel, it was only about a mile and half until the top of the grade at 2,072 feet was reached, just before the track entered Alleghany tunnel, which took it under the ridge and into West Virginia. In between Alleghany and Lewis tunnels was the tiny town and station of Alleghany. The C&O built a station here and put in a turntable which was used to turn locomotives being used as pushers from either direction. It was quite a busy settlement in the late 19th and early 20th century and crews sometimes laid over. The station handled a good traffic in agricultural products and implements.

By the 1890s C&O's operations included adding a pusher locomotive at Ronceverte, W. Va., at the base of the grade on the west slope, which pushed the train to Alleghany, cut off and ran light back to Ronceverte. Sometime in the 1930s, it is believed, the pusher operation was moved so that coal trains leaving Hinton were pushed all the way to Alleghany. In the later decades of steam, first the big H-7 2-8-8-2s were used, one as the road engine and one pushing, and then in the early 1940s the H-8 2-6-6-6s completely supplanted them. The turntable at Alleghany was 115-feet, which was just enough to accommodate the H-7 or H-8.

About 1905 Alleghany Tunnel was enlarged for a second track, but by the 1920, the larger equipment caused clearance problems, so as part of the big tunnel improvement program the new Alleghany Tunnel bore was completed in 1932, and the old one was converted to single track as well.

Today (2011) one track has been taken up from OX cabin west of Callaghan to the summit, eliminating the old bore at Lewis Tunnel, and the double track picks up at that point through Alleghany and through both bores at Alleghany Tunnel.

Profile of Alleghany Subdivision, showing entire line Clifton Forge, Va. to Hinton, W. Va. - The state line is in Alleghany Tunnel. (C&O Historical Society Collection)

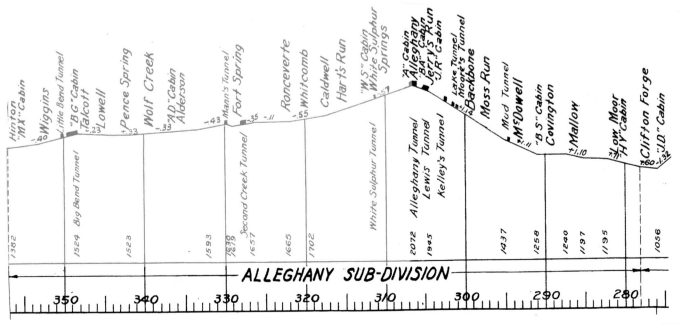

At Lewis Tunnel there was a "bad air" problem in the steam era. To help this a giant fan was placed which blew a strong draft in the direction of the train's westward travel, so that it kept the exhaust gases in front of the train. If one were positioned at the west portal of the westbound bore at Lewis, a big cloud of smoke would emerge from the tunnel long before the train itself. The only other operation such as this on the C&O was at Big Bend Tunnel, at Talcott, W. Va., also on the Alleghany Subdivision.

This part of the subdivision really had only one important station, Covington. This is the seat of Alleghany County and as such always had a good business to contribute to the C&O's traffic. In 1900 the West Virginia Pulp and Paper Company built a paper mill here. It grew over the decades and is today one of the largest paper mills east of the Mississippi River, and provides a large business to CSX today, as it did to C&O the years before. Another plant, the Industrial Rayon Corporation, was built near the town in the 1928. It was a big customer for many decades, and during World War II traffic to and from the plant was huge, with 1,000 people employed. It closed in 1960 and some of the buildings were later used by the Hercules Corporation to make fiber products. Covington is the location where both the Hot Springs and Potts Creek branches terminated.

At Backbone station, not far from Lewis Tunnel on the eastern slope, an iron ore mine was established and supplied traffic to C&O via a connecting narrow gauge railroad up to the early 1900s.

The eastern terminal of the Alleghany Subdivision was Clifton Forge (see chapter 10) which was C&O's second largest shop area, and one of its largest yards and operational points.

The Alleghany grade eastbound was only 0.56% from Ronceverte to Alleghany, which was the direction for the flow of coal, and this was the operating reality that C&O built most of its steam motive power to accommodate. From Alleghany west the line passed White Sulphur Springs where the C&O owned Greenbrier Resort Hotel. It passed through several small towns with agricultural business, several tunnels, and finally reached Hinton, at the confluence of the Greenbrier and New Rivers. The total mileage of the line is 77.8 miles, of which about 30 are in Virginia.

The Hot Springs Branch

The Hot Springs Subdivision was built in 1890-91 from Covington up the Warms Springs Valley to Hot Springs station. It was the only branch C&O ever built which was mainly to handle passenger traffic. It seems that when M. E. Ingalls assumed the presidency of the C&O in 1889, as the Morgans and Vanderbilts took over, he toured the line and was enamored of the "Springs of the Virginias." He tried to buy the White Sulphur Springs hotel and grounds but it was unavailable, so he instead purchased the hotel at Hot

Springs, and built a grand new brick structure there called the Homestead. It became one of the major resort hotels in America in the 20th Century. Though C&O had a share of ownership in the hotel, Ingalls and his family eventually took complete control, and it was owned by his family up into the 1990s.

Ingalls had a railway to bring passengers to his new hotel, but at its closest point it was 25 miles away at Covington, so he had C&O build the 24.7-mile Hot Springs Branch. Through Pullman cars originated in New York and brought passengers from there, Philadelphia, Baltimore, and Washington to Clifton Forge, where they were removed from the mainline trains and taken up the branch by passenger trains operating Clifton Forge-Covington-Hot Springs. At its height the line had eight trains per day, meeting all mainline trains. Over time, as the business declined, the branch was reduced to a single train each day which ran as a mixed train, carrying the sleeping cars from the mainline as well as any freight for the line, which usually was only a car or two of coal. This lasted until the last through sleepers were discontinued in 1970. Soon after that the line was taken up for several miles out of Hot Springs, while part of it was used for a few years as a tourist steam railroad. After a few years this business closed and the entire line was taken up in the late 1970s. [For a complete story of *Resort Special* trains to the Homestead and Greenbrier see the Holiday 2007 issue of the *C&O Historical Magazine*, available and from the C&O Historical Society (chessieshop.com)]

Potts Creek Branch

The Potts Creek Branch was built for a distance of 20 miles between Covington and Bess between 1906 and 1908, largely at the request of the Low Moor Iron Company of Low Moor and Covington, to open what was believed to be very large iron ore deposits for use by the company's two furnaces. Low Moor Company estimated that it would be able to extract 25,000,000 tons of ore, and it agreed to ship 3,200,000 tons in the first 15 years. Other than the iron ore, the line had no other resources, and was very rural in nature.

In fact, the iron ore was not as good as expected and the iron business in the region went into a steady decline as large rich deposits in the western United States supplanted the relatively small resources of Virginia. Thus the line was never profitable for the C&O. It was abandoned except for the first 3.5 miles beyond Covington. This portion was renamed the "Potts Creek Industrial Spur," and was used to reach the new Industrial Rayon Company plant at this location. This portion of the line remains in place as of this writing.

Motive Power

The heaviest and most powerful steam locomotives built for the C&O were used on the Alleghany Subdivision throughout its history. In the 1870s the line was populated by the small 4-4-0 and 4-6-0 types that comprised the C&O's whole fleet, carrying cars of 20-tons or less capacity. As coal deposits opened and trains became heavier C&O bought 2-8-0 Consolidation types beginning in 1881 and built increasingly heavier and more powerful types of this wheel arrangement through 1909, when its G-9 class reached the limit to which this type of locomotive could be expanded.

In 1911 C&O acquired its first 2-6-6-2 compound articulated Mallet type for use on the coal trains over the 0.56% 13-mile eastbound Alleghany grade from Hinton to Alleghany. By the early 1920s there were hundreds of this type in operation which greatly relieved the congestion of trains on the Alleghany Subdivision. In 1905 Clifton Forge yard was receiving about 1,000 cars per day, in trains of 40-50 cars per train, with two 2-8-0s as motive power. This required

The impressive station at Covington was erected in about 1906 and was a very close copy of the one that was built at about this time at Staunton (see page 90). The building at the left is the passenger station built in 1889. When the new passenger structure was built it became the express facility. Canopies covered both east and westbound platforms. The station has been beautifully restored today, but the canopies are gone. (C&O Ry. Photo, C&O Historical Society Collection, CSPR-10393.099)

20 trains, with about ¾ that many empties westbound, plus through and local freights and passenger trains. The Mallets allowed the coal trains to increase in size, resulting in fewer trains to haul more coal.

In 1924-35 the giant H-7 simple articulated 2-8-8-2 H-7 class arrived and took over the heavy coal business. They were the kings of the Alleghany grade until 1942 when the H-8 2-6-6-6s supplanted them. By that time 125 50-ton cars could be lifted from Hinton to Alleghany by an H-8 on the front and another on the rear.

All coal trains stopped at Alleghany where they dropped the pusher (which turned and went back to Hinton), and at East Alleghany where retainers were set up for the steep down-grade run east. The train stopped again just west of Covington where the retainers were turned back down before it proceeded on to Clifton Forge.

Manifest freights were handled by 2-8-2s in the 1920s and in the 1930s by those or H-7s. From 1942 to the end of steam manifest freights had H-8s. Local freights got 2-8-2s usually, and sometimes 2-8-4s after they began to arrive in 1943, until the end of steam on his Subdivision in 1954. K-4s handled manifest freights during this period as well. When a particularly heavy westbound manifest left Clifton Forge it would be pushed to Alleghany. This operation usually consisted of a K-4 on each end.

For passenger trains the 4-4-0s and 4-6-0s were supplanted by 4-4-2s and 4-6-2s in 1902. From that point onward the heaviest of C&O's passenger engines were used on this line. The 4-6-2 Pacific types got heavier and more powerful through the F-19 classes of 1926, and were regulars on this run. The 4-8-2s were developed by C&O in 1911 and in addition to handling trains over the Mountain Subdivision between Charlottesville and Clifton Forge, they were power for trains between Clifton Forge and Hinton. The final development of passenger power began in 1935 when the J-3 class 4-8-4 Greenbrier types arrived. These locomotives either ran through Chlotttesville-Hinton, or only or one leg or the other based on availability. Two more came in 1942 and a final five in 1948.

Dieselization began with switch engines and then GP7s and GP9s, so that by 1954 steam was gone east of Alleghany. Passenger trains were completely dieselized with E8 model units between August 1951 and January 1952. For a while, displaced 4-8-4s were used as pushers out of Hinton to Alleghany.

Today coal trains and the two remaining through freights get the back-to-back pairs of high horsepower CSX units, and the 6-7-car *Cardinal* Amtrak passenger trains have a single one of that company's Genesis units.

Traffic

As alluded to before, the principal traffic on this line was coal east and empty coal cars west, in the 1940s-1950s amounting to as many as twelve 125 car trains per day each way. In the mid-20th Century era of this book, two sets of manifest freights operated, as well as a local way freight each way each day. All mainline passenger trains, of course, passed over the line. In 1949 this consisted of three sets of name train, *The George Washington* (Nos. 1 and 2), *The Sportsman* (Nos. 4 & 5), *The Fast Flying Virginian* (Nos. 3 and 6), as well as main and express only trains 103 and 104, and passenger locals 13 and 14 (Nos. 14 and 104 were consolidated in 1949). Nos. 104 and 13 were cut off in the fall of 1958. Nos. 5 and 6 were discontinued in the Fall of 1962, and Nos. 3 and 4 were eliminated in May 1968. Nos. 1 & 2 remained until Amtrak day May 1, 1971. Subsequently Amtrak ran one daily train each way until it was cut back to three days per week (which is the operation as of this writing).

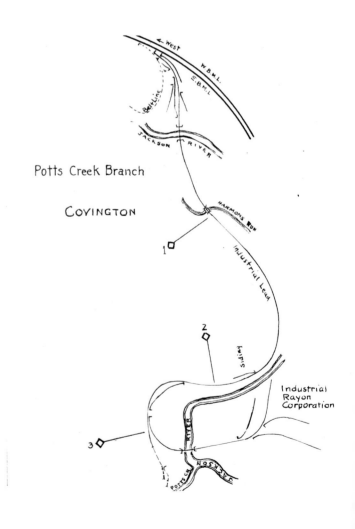

Opposite Below and Right: These side track maps show the Covington yard, which accommodated the business for the town including the large freight station (bottom of the map), and all the cars that were being staged in and out of the paper mill, as well as the belt line spur that led to numerous sidings and the stub end of the Potts Creek Branch leading to the Rayon plant, 3.9 miles from the station. (C&O Historical Society Collection)

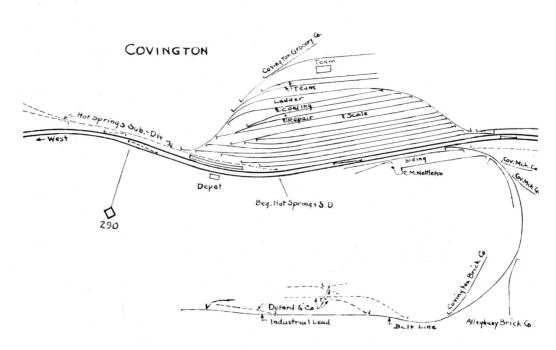

Map of Potts Creek Branch after its retirement. (C&O Historical Society Collection)

Map of Hot Springs Branch. (C&O Historical Society Collection)

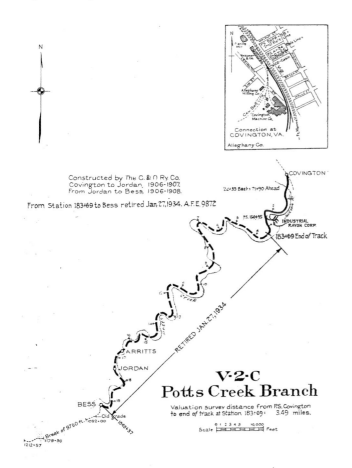

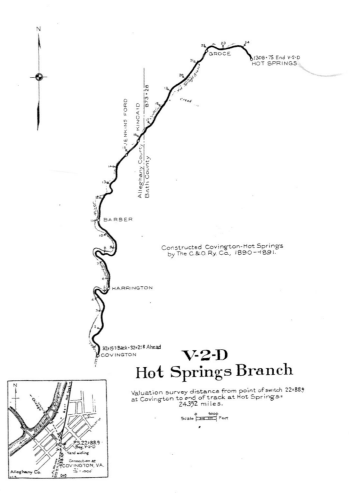

The Hot Springs mixed train is seen at the Hot Springs station with its unusual consist of a GP7, 11-double bedroom Pullman, heavyweight combination car, empty hopper and wooden caboose on March 9, 1968, near the end of its life. The Pullman has just delivered its New York passengers to the Homestead Hotel. They just walked across the road from this point. The hotel's steam plant is behind the station and is the reason for the hopper. (T. W. Dixon, Jr. Photo, C&O Historical Society Collection)

The Homestead Hotel at Hot Springs, destination point for so much of C&O passenger business in the era 1890-1969. (C&O Ry. Photo, C&O Historical Society Collection, CSPR-2909)

Smoke from the Covington paper mill can be seen rising above the trees as we see C&O Train No. 5/47, The Sportsman, with two E8s and 16 cars heading west at McDowell, a few miles west of Covington, on its way toward Detroit and Cincinnati in the summer of 1956. Ahead is the climb up the east slope of Alleghany Mountain. (C&O Ry. Photo, C&O Historical Society Collection, CSPR-10393.103)

A favorite photo point just west of Covington was at Moss Run. Seen there in 1959, five GP7s and GP9s have an empty coal train. The diesels took over all operations east of Alleghany in 1954, and all steam was gone by 1955.(C&O Ry. Photo, C&O Historical Society Collection, CSPR-4578)

Taken 10 years earlier than the previous photo, these official 1949 photos show the peak of steam locomotion on the Alleghany grade. H-8 2-6-6-6 No. 1654 is headed west with a big train of empties as it assaults the grade. The giant H-8s were the exclusive power for both coal and freight trains both ways over the Alleghany Subdivision. (C&O Ry. Photo, C&O Historical Society Collection, CSPR-2232, 2229)

An eastbound coal train with a brace of three GP7/9s is on the big fill at Jerry's Run with an eastbound coal train. When the diesels first came three units were used as the road engine and a steam locomotive was the pusher Hinton-Alleghany. Once steam was gone, five units were put up front and the pusher eliminated, only to be reinstated until the late 1970s, and then only Ronceverte-Alleghany. (C&O Historical Society Collection)

H-8 No. 1652 is headed west out of the "old" Lewis Tunnel at East Alleghany in 1950. (H. W. Pontin Photo, C&O Historical Society Collection, COHS-1137)

In the summer of 1952 and the twilight of steam, K-2 2-8-2 No. 1245 is pausing at Alleghany station with a local freight as K-4 No. 2762 passes pushing a westbound manifest freight train. Pushers out of Clifton Forge were used only if a fast freight had a particularly heavy train. In these cases a K-4 was used as the road engine and another K-4 as the pusher. H-8s would not normally have a pusher westbound. (B. F. Cutler Photo, C&O Historical Society Collection)

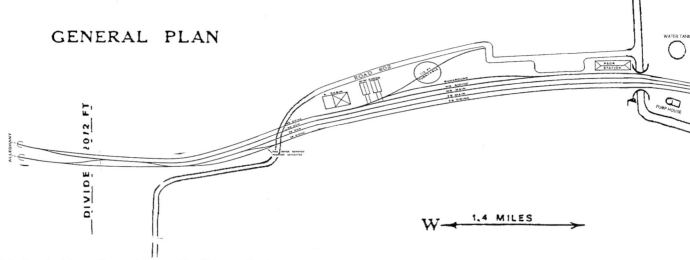

GENERAL PLAN

This drawing shows the trackage and facilities at Alleghany *(From the book* Alleghany With an A, *C&O Historical Society, 1989)*

H-8 No. 1601 is headed west with a manifest freight passing A Cabin at Alleghany. It will soon enter Alleghany Tunnel and West Virginia. Another H-8 with an empty coal train is in the rear. The typical C&O cantilever signal tower was just removed in 2009. (C&O Ry. Photo, C&O Historical Society Collection)

ALLEGHANY   1945

ALT 2070

WATER TANK

PUMP HOUSE

STATE HIGHWAY 311

LEWIS

SCALE IS APPROXIMATE

The photographer is in A Cabin is looking east toward the station, water tank, stock pens, turntable, and section tool house at Alleghany in 1947. (Bruce Fales Photo, Jay Williams Collection)

In August 1948 H-8 1605 has just un-coupled after pushing an eastbound coal train from Hinton. The caboose behind the tender will be reattached to the coal train and the H-8 turned for its trip back to Hinton light. (B. F. Cutler Photo, C&O Historical Society Collection, COHS-1515)

A westbound freight is about to enter the new bore at Alleghany Tunnel in 1946 with a fast freight . The old bore at left was double tracked in 1905, but as bigger equipment came into use, a new tunnel had to be dug to the right in 1932 to avoid a bottleneck. (J. I. Kelly Photo, C&O Historical Society Collection (COHS-9569)

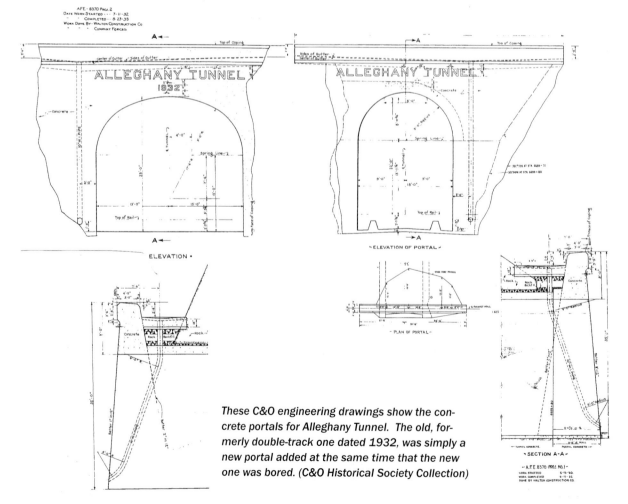

These C&O engineering drawings show the concrete portals for Alleghany Tunnel. The old, formerly double-track one dated 1932, was simply a new portal added at the same time that the new one was bored. (C&O Historical Society Collection)

12: Passenger Service

Although passenger trains and their operations and motive power are treated throughout this book, this short chapter is intended to give the reader a "big picture" look at the overall system of trains C&O operated within Virginia. The era of our treatment is 1949.

C&O passenger train operations in Virginia were still at a high level in 1949, even though the additional service that had been established in 1943 to accommodate World War II traffic, had been cut off in 1948 after the post-war boom in traffic declined. After 1950, passenger operations on the C&O in and in America were in steady decline until the remaining trains were taken over the National Railroad Passenger Corporation: Amtrak.

As has been discussed in previous chapters of this book, the overall system of C&O passenger train operations before and after WWII was as follows: Trains originated at Cincinnati and traveled over the Cincinnati Division to Ashland, Kentucky. Another "Kentucky Section" of most trains started at Louisville at about the same time, came up through Lexington and met the Cincinnati-origin train at Ashland. (*The Sportsman* was the exception. Its sections ran Ashland-Cincinatti and Ashland-Drtroit, with no Kentucky section.) Here the consists of the two trains were combined and adjusted, and the combined train was sent eastward across West Virginia and a part of Virginia. At Charlottesville, cars for the "Virginia Section" of the train were cut out of the consist and sent down the Piedmont Subdivision to Richmond and over the Peninsula Subdivision to Newport News. The rest of the train was sent on to Washington via the Washington Subdivision trackage rights over the Southern Railway. The operation simply reversed westbound.

Some cars terminated or were added at Charlottesville, and some local trains terminated and originated there, so there was always a need for a coach yard to hold these and other extra cars. A coach yard was a bit different from an ordinary yard in that the tracks had to have electrical outlets so that the cars could be plugged in to "standby power" to operate their systems and charge their batteries when they were not moving on a train. Likewise, steam connections were needed to keep static cars warm during cold weather. Other coach yards were at Hot Springs, Clifton Forge, Richmond, and Phoebus (later Newport News).

Normally, when an eastbound train arrived at Charlottesville, the motive power (in the steam days) was taken to the engine terminal and after the Virginia Section was made up it would leave. A few minutes later the Washington section would depart. In the opposite direction the Virginia section usually arrived first and then was combined with the Washington Section when it arrived, for the trip west.

In addition to being a primary location for passenger car adjustment, storage, and cleaning, Charlottesville also had a branch of the C&O's commissary department which supplied food and supplies to dining cars. The main commissary was at Ashland, Ky. in the west. C&O operated its dining cars in such a way that they often were on the train only when they were needed to serve a meal. In this way fewer cars could cover the system, and Charlottesville was often the staging area for diners. Many cooks lived here.

J-2 4-8-2 Mountain type No. 545 is seen here with Train No. 5, The Sportsman near Alexandria in 1942, with a consist of five head end cars (including a full RPO) and six passenger-carrying cars. Typical of a heavy Washington section. Traffic was so heavy during the war that second sections had to operated out of Charlottesville. This was regularized in August 1943, when C&O stopped combining the trains and simply ran each section through, one behind the other by about 30 minutes. This lasted until October 1948. (Wayne Kendricks Photo)

F-16 Pacific is poised to take Train No. 141 west from Phoebus at 2:15 pm, February 22, 1946, with a consist of an express car, RPO, express car, baggage car, regular coach, and two Imperial Salon coaches. No. 141 at this time ran as far as Gordonsville for local work. Passengers could transfer there to other through trains. (R. R. Malinoski Photo)

When the Louisa Railroad first decided to cancel its contract for the RF&P to run its trains, it took special care to buy a couple of "state-of-the-art" coaches for 1847, though they were very crude by later standards. In 1850 Virginia Central had trains running from Richmond to Charlottesville, and by 1857 the line was extended to Jackson's River Station (near present Clifton Forge), where stages met the trains. The stages took passengers on to the Virginia and West Virginia springs resorts or along the JR&K Turnpike all the way to the Ohio River. In 1869 trains began operating into White Sulphur Springs, about 5 miles over the West Virginia line, and in May 1873 through operation to Huntington, W. Va. was established, with riverboat connections to Cincinnati. After 1881 rail connections to Cincinnati were available over other roads owned by C. P. Huntington. Then, 1889 the C&O's Cincinnati Division was completed along the Kentucky side of the Ohio River and across that river into the Queen City. In the same year C&O negotiated trackage rights over the Virginia Midland (later Southern, now Norfolk Southern) from Orange into Washington (also using short stretches of RF&P and PRR trackage). This set the stage for passenger operations for the next 80 years, whereby the Washington-Cincinnati section of mainline would be the most important passenger carrying line. The old Charlottesville-Newport News line was a connector as well as the Ashland-Lexington-Louisville (via L&N trackage rights) and Ashland-Detroit were in the west.

Through passenger business from the great eastern cities was courted from the beginning, and passengers from those cites to Hot Springs and White Sulphur Springs became an important element in C&O passenger operations. In 1949 considerable dedicated Pullman traffic originated in New York and terminated at Clifton Forge for transport to Hot Springs, or at White Sulphur Springs. Similar traffic originated in the west, but to a much smaller degree that the New York trade.

In 1949 the following sleeping cars originated or terminated in Virginia:

Train No. 41/1 - *The George Washington*
Phoebus to Chicago (via NYC from Cincinnati)
Phoebus to St. Louis (via NYC from Cincinnati)

Train No. 2/42 - *The George Washington*
Cincinnati to Phoebus
St. Louis to Phoebus (via NYC St. Louis-Cincinnati)

Train No. 43/3, *The Fast Flying Virginian* (FFV)
Phoebus to Huntington
Phoebus to Chicago (via NYC from Cincinnati)

Train No. 6 - *The FFV*
Hot Springs to New York

Train No. 5/47 - *The Sportsman*
Phoebus to Detroit
Phoebus to Chicago (via Toledo and NKP)
Clifton Forge to Cleveland (via NKP) (for White Sulphur Springs traffic)

Train No. 4/46 - *The Sportsman*
Chicago to Phoebus
Detroit to Phoebus

Cleveland to Clifton Forge (for White Sulphur Springs traffic)

Two things should be noted from this list: cars originating at terminating in Virginia were either at the eastern terminal for the Virginia sections at Phoebus, or they originated/terminated at Hot Springs or at Clifton Forge for White Sulphur Springs business. Through cars carrying other passengers for points in Virginia were on a run terminating or beginning in Washington.

At this point it should be explained why the cars are shown as originating and terminating at Phoebus, on the Hampton Branch (see Chapter 1) rather than at Newport News. In fact, C&O advertised its eastern passenger terminal points a Newport News, Norfolk, and Phoebus!

During this era and up until 1957, C&O trains actually originated and terminated at Phoebus, Milepost 1. The cars were kept there and locomotives were serviced and turned between runs 12 miles up the line at Newport News' engine terminal. The train would leave Phoebus westbound, arrive at Old Point Junction where it intersected the Newport News yard. It would then back about a mile to the Newport News passenger station and pier. Here the steamer from Portsmouth and Norfolk would deliver passengers over the pier (until 1951 when a bus replaced the ferry). The train would then head west. For eastbound trains, the train would pull into Newport News, then back to Old Point Junction, and thence head down the Hampton Branch to Phoebus, and the whole process would be repeated. In 1957 this operation was eliminated. C&O built a platform and canopy at Old Point Junction. From that time forward trains simply originated at terminated at Newport News station and then stopped at the new platform which was called Hampton Roads Transfer, where a bus from Phoebus transferred passengers from Ft. Monroe, Phoebus, and Hampton. This saved a huge amount of time, effort, and facilities.

Looking at the January 16, 1949, timetable that is the basis for this chapter's study, we find that in addition the three sets of name trains, there were several local passenger trains. Between Charlottesville and Richmond three trains operated: Nos. 3, 44, and 116 eastbound and from Richmond to Charlottesville one train, No. 141. The exact reason or this imbalance isn't clear, but one of these trains was certainly to take care of a slot that was not filled because No. 6 did not have a Virginia Section. Certainly No. 44 was a commuter train for Richmond, leaving Charlottes-ville at 4:30 am and arriving Richmond at 8:00 am. Likewise 141 left Richmond at 5:30 pm arriving Charlottesville at 7:25 pm. These trains had regular or flag stops at 20 stations on the Piedmont Subdivision.

No. 13 was the mainline local westbound from Charlottesville, originating there at 6:25 am and terminating Huntington, W. Va. at 6:50 pm. The eastbound local was No. 104, which originated at Huntington at 3:45 am and terminated at Charlottesville at 4:25 pm.

On the Peninsula Subdivision no local trains operated, but No. 48 left Richmond at 7:00 pm, arriving Phoebus at 9:15. This train had no westbound counterpart. It is thought that this was to ferry equipment to Phoebus since No. 6 didn't have a Virginia section.

East of Charlottesville, the name train sets operated over the Piedmont Subdivision about 20 miles to Gordonsville and took the Washington Subdivision from that point, then from Orange over trackage rights on the Southern mainline, a short stretch of the RF&P and PRR into Washington Union Terminal. There all coaches and head-end cars terminated and through Pullmans were attached to PRR trains to New York. No local passenger trains operated on this line.

In the years following 1949 this system slowly shrank. First, Nos. 13 and 104 were cut off in 1958, the in October 1962 Nos. 6 and 5/47 were eliminated. In May 1968 Nos. 4/46 and 43/3 were cut off leaving only Nos. 2/42 and 41/1, *The George Washington*, which lasted to Amtrak day, May 1, 1971. At that time Amtrak began operating a single daily train from Newport News to Cincinnati with a connection from Washington, but this was soon reversed with the bigger of the trains originating and terminating in Washington and a connection to Newport News as in the C&O days. The western terminal varied from Cincinnati to Chicago. From Ocober 1, 1981 until January 8, 1982 the train was cut off and here was no passenger service on the old C&O main line. When it was restored it operated only three days per week. Now named the *Cardinal*, it is still on a three days per week schedule as of this writing. Connections from Richmond are by bus to Charlottesville.

In the early 1980s Amtrak added service originating in Washington to Richmond via the RF&P, thence over the C&O to Newport News. This has increased in volume and currently 8 trains operate in this service, stopping at Richmond, Williamsburg, and Newport News on the C&O. The Amtrak station at Newport News is a new structure that was built on the site of C&O's old Hampton Roads Transfer station.

Branch Line Passenger Trains

James River Line (James River and Rivanna Subdivisions) Clifton Forge-Richmond via Lynchburg

Train No. 9 (Daily)		Train No. 10 (Daily)	
Lv. Richmond	7:10 am	Lv. Clifton Forge	8:37 am
Ar. Clifton Forge	3:50 pm	Ar. Richmond	5:05 pm
Train No. 33 (Daily except Sunday)		**Train No. 34 (Daily except Sunday)**	
Lv. Lynchburg	7:00 am	Lv. Clifton Forge	3:45 pm
Ar. Clifton Forge	10:10 am	Ar. Lynchburg	7:10 pm

These trains were operated by Brill Gas-electric motor cars with a trailing car.

Virginia Air Line Subdivision

No. 403 (Mixed Train Ex. Sunday)		No. 404 (Mixed Train Ex. Sunday)	
Lv. Gordonsville	2:10 pm	Lv. Strathmore	7:00 am
Ar. Strathmore	3:15 pm	Ar. Gordonsville	8:40 am

Buckingham Branch

No. 307 (Mixed Train Ex. Sunday)		No. 308 (Mixed Train Ex. Sunday)	
Lv. Bremo	9:45 am	Lv. Dillwyn	12:10 pm
Ar. Dillwyn	11:00 am	Ar. Bremo	1:20 pm

Lexington Branch

Train No. 200 (Mixed Train Ex. Sunday)		Train No. 201 (Mixed Train Ex. Sunday)	
Lv. Balcony Falls	8:00 am	Lv. Lexington	9:30 am
Ar. Lexington	9:25 am	Ar. Balcony Falls	12:30 pm

Craig Valley Branch

Train No. 109 (Mixed Train M & Th)		Train No. 108 (Mixed Train M & Th)	
Lv. Eagle Rock	11:00 am	Lv. New Castle	2:00 pm
Ar. New Castle	12:50 am	Ar. Eagle Rock	3:30 pm

Alberene Branch

Train No. 209 (Mixed Train Ex. Sunday)		Train No. 210 (Mixed Train Ex. Sunday)	
Lv. Warren	1:50 pm	Lv. Esmont	13:45 pm
Ar. Esmont	2:15 pm	Ar. Warren	1:10 pm

Hot Springs Branch

	No. 303	No. 305		No. 310	No. 306
	Daily	Mixed Daily		Mixed Daily	Daily
Lv. C. Forge	6:15 am	2:00 pm	Lv. Hot Spgs.	8:45 am	8:15 pm
Ar Hot Spgs.	8:10 am	4:00 pm	Ar. C. Forge	10:35 am	9:45 pm

In addition to the mainline trains, C&O was still operating numerous branch line local service in 1949 as shown on the opposite page.

Branch line trains were discontinued by the mid-1950s, with the James River Line local ending Oct. 27, 1957. Only a single mixed train survived, on the Hot Springs Branch. It still carried sleeping cars dropped by the name trains at Clifton Forge to Hot Springs and returned them after leaving the passengers there. These trains were finally discontinued in 1970 after the last through Hot Springs Pullmans ran in the fall of 1969.

However, trains that were not listed in the public timetable also operated at night. It was essentially a switching operation whereby a locomotive from Clifton Forge would gather sleepers at Hot Springs and from White Sulphur Springs, and bring them back to be attached to No. 2 in the early hours of the morning at Clifton Forge.

During the summer in the 1960s, C&O also operated a *Resort Special* train that originated at Clifton Forge, picked up cars at White Sulphur Springs, and passengers at Covington (by limousine from Hot Springs), and operated through to Washington as a special train during the "season" several days per week.

Clifton Forge had an extensive coach yard where special movement cars were stored and serviced after having arrived with special parties for Hot Springs or White Sulphur Springs. Very often foreign road cars would be present here, most often Pennsylvania, with some NYC and other roads mixed in more occasionally.

An extra E8 was usually stationed at Clifton Forge in the 1960s for use on special movements and *Resort Specials*. Steam-generator-equipped GP7s were also used in these services.

E8 4027 with No. 41 is parked on what was left of the passenger pier at Newport News. It will soon head west on this February 7, 1971, just three months before Amtrak. Locomotives could not go out on the pier. (T. W. Dixon, Jr. Photo)

C&O built a platform and canopy at Old Point Junction which it called Hampton Roads Transfer. Here buses from Ft. Monroe, Phoebus, and Hampton met the trains after the railway discontinued sending trains down the Hampton branch to originate and terminate at Phoebus. In this late days photo the operation is still in effect. No. 41 is on the platform. The truck at right has just loaded some newspapers. This was Feb. 2, 1970, just a little over a year before the advent of Amtrak. (T. W. Dixon, Jr. Photo)

E-units were constantly parked at the Charlottesville engine terminal between runs, and one or two were usually kept here to "protect" for specials or mechanical problems on the regular runs. This photo of No. 4019 still in the old colors was taken June 13, 1970. (T. W. Dixon, Jr. Photo)

Double-headed out of Staunton with two passenger-equipped K-4 2-8-4 Kanawhas (2763 and 2761) a heavy train makes its way west near Swoope, ready to assault the North Mountain grade in about 1949. (C&O Ry. Photo, C&O Historical Society Collection, CSPR-2356)

No. 13, the local, has 4-8-2 No. 543 and four cars westbound leaving Crozet station in July 1948. The express car up front and the combination RPO/Express/baggage car next accounted for a lot of the revenue for this train. One wonders how many people populated the combine and coach, even in this era. (J. I. Kelly Photo, C&O Historical Society Collection, COHS-90)

Last run of No. 6, the eastbound *Fast Flying Virginian* was captured by photographer Bill Warden as its E8 4015 nosed into Waynesboro on October 28 1962. It was due at Waynesboro at 11:08 pm, but must have been late because it is running as an extra (see white flags), since No 6 was annulled and discontinued as of midnight. (W. E. Warden, Jr. Photo)

C&O bought three giant M-1 class steam-turbine-electrics for use on C&O Chairman Robert R. Young's pet project, The Chessie, an all coach daylight Cincinnati-Washington train. However, the train was cancelled and the M-1s were worked for about a year on regular trains. Here No. 501 has No. 4, The Sportsman, running east of Clifton Forge in January 1949. Soon after this the turbines were scrapped as failures in the face of dieselization. The train has 10 cars, but No. 46 is running as a second section about 30 minutes later according to the photographer's notes. (Gene Huddleston Photo)

The Hot Springs mixed train is about ready to leave Clifton Forge with a box car, combination car, a lightweight Pennsylvania RR sleeper, and a Pullman pool car in October 1954. (J. R. Kean Photo, C&O Historical Society Collection, COHS-3375)

Opposite: These two photos taken in 1959 at Griffith, just east of Clifton Forge, very well illustrate the composition of C&O passenger trains in the late 1950s era between Clifton Forge and Charlottesville. The mail/express/local trains were cut in 1958 and a lot of head-end business was added to the name trains. Here No. 4, The Sportsman, has three E8s, eight head end cars, and nine passenger cars. The consist is obviously swollen by a special movement of some type because of the two heavyweight coaches ahead of the diner. (C&O Ry. Photo, C&O Historical Society Collection, CSPR-234565, 4579)

The little mixed train with its litter motive power is seen here on the Nelson & Albemarle at Esmont. C&O owned the line as part of its Alberene branch but N&A operated it. (University of Virginia Collection)

The Buckingham Branch mixed train is seen here leaving Dillwyn on November 11, 1950, with pulpwood and other mixed freight as its wooden combine brings up the rear. (J. I. Kelly Photo, D. Wallace Johnson Collection)

Brill gas-electric (by this time converted to diesel) No. 9053 is seen on a rainy day in December 1954 working mail and express at Lynchburg Union Station. Train No. 9 consisted of the stout Brill car and a trailer and had left Richmond at 6:00 am, reaching Lynchburg at 10:48. After a ten minute station stop, it was off to Clifton Forge. It had 10 scheduled and 32 flag stops on the 231 miles between Richmond ad Clifton Forge—a true local. (TLC Collection)